CONFLICT AND DECISION MAKING IN ELEMENTARY SCHOOLS

Contemporary Vignettes and Cases for School Administrators

Dennis C. Zuelke

H-Z Consultants, Ltd.

Marvin Willerman

Northeastern Illinois University

WCB **Wm. C. Brown Publishers**

Book Team

Editor *Paul L. Tavenner*
Production Coordinator *Carla D. Arnold*

Wm. C. Brown Publishers

President *G. Franklin Lewis*
Vice President, Publisher *Thomas E. Doran*
Vice President, Operations and Production *Beverly Kolz*
National Sales Manager *Virginia S. Moffat*
Group Sales Manager *Eric Ziegler*
Executive Editor *Edgar J. Laube*
Director of Marketing *Kathy Law Laube*
Marketing Manager *Pamela S. Cooper*
Managing Editor, Production *Colleen A. Yonda*
Manager of Visuals and Design *Faye M. Schilling*
Production Editorial Manager *Julie A. Kennedy*
Production Editorial Manager *Ann Fuerste*
Publishing Services Manager *Karen J. Slaght*

WCB Group

President and Chief Executive Officer *Mark C. Falb*
Chairman of the Board *Wm. C. Brown*

Cover photo by Sue Markson

Cover and interior design by Stuart D. Paterson

Copyedited by Maureen Peifer

Library of Congress Catalog Card Number: 91–71407

ISBN 0–697–14002–4

Printed in the United States of America by Wm. C. Brown Publishers,
2460 Kerper Boulevard, Dubuque, IA 52001

10 9 8 7 6 5 4 3 2 1

To my parents, Gladys
and Clarence Zuelke
D. C. Z.

To my wife, Barbara Willerman
M. W.

CONTENTS

CHAPTER 7

CHAPTER 8

ACKNOWLEDGMENTS

Go the distance.
W. P. Kinsella

The authors wish to acknowledge the many students of educational administration who have shared with them anecdotes of their experiences that were instrumental in the writing of this book. Special gratitude is reserved for Daniel Rice of the University of North Dakota for his fine research and writing contributions to the original edition of this book. We thank former Associate Dean Cecelia Traugh and former Dean Vito Perrone, Center for Teaching and Learning, University of North Dakota for making funds available so that work on the original edition of this book could move ahead. We also thank Robert King of the University of North Dakota who so expertly edited portions of our original manuscript. We would like to acknowledge the reviewers who worked with us on this edition: Jack Klotz from Indiana University, Donald K. Lemon from the University of North Dakota, G. Keith Dolan from California State University, W. Lou Shields from Houston Baptist University, Peter J. Burke from Wisconsin Department of Public Instruction, and David R. Friedman from the University of Wisconsin. Finally, we wish to thank Stella Kocher who painstakingly typed and retyped the original manuscript as we made changes and Karen Rausch for her diligent word processing efforts as we revised and updated portions of the book.

Dennis C. Zuelke   Marvin Willerman
H-Z Consultants, Ltd. Northeastern Illinois University
Superior, WI   Chicago

SEPT 1991

INTRODUCTION

The main source for the dilemmas
leaders face can be found within
themselves, in their own inner conflicts.
Abraham Zaleznik

Elementary school principals face serious challenges to their leadership position in contemporary American education. Teachers may differ in their expectations of the principal's role, parents may misconceive it, school district offices may disagree with it, and general criticisms may undermine it. Because of these challenges, conflict may be commonplace in many elementary schools. A point may be reached where school resources in time, funds, and mental and emotional energy are inordinately taxed and diverted to resolve conflict. Tension, anxiety, and hard feelings, permeating among members of the school community, can make supporting and trusting relationships impossible.

Conflict as such, however, is not necessarily detrimental to the school, and the proper management of conflict will change the school into a better teaching-learning environment. It is important for principals and administrators to realize this. At a time of national investigatory reports and heightened public scrutiny of education, the elementary principal's ability to manage conflict and make decisions is more crucial now to the success of the school than in years past.

First we should understand what resources principals have to work with. In order to manage conflict and to make decisions, principals have to rely mainly on a combination of three types of authority or influence: position, referent, and expert. Position authority is simply the authority inherent in one's official position or office. Referent influence is the ability to influence or persuade others because they respect or identify with the administrator, and expert influence results from the administrator's work-related knowledge and skill.

Principals in conflict, of course, cannot rely solely on position authority or personal influence. They are becoming more aware that where no legal precedents or policy guidelines are established, they must make their decisions in the light of common sense and group consensus. If a principal's position authority becomes suspect, rational decision making becomes extremely important. Often the rationality of a decision is judged by its results, but there may be many results of a single decision. Assume that one principal unilaterally decides on a new reading program while another uses a collaborative process with the faculty and acquires community support for that reading program. Assume further that the personally chosen program shows higher student achievement. Which principal is the better decision maker? Although higher student achievement may be seen as the main goal of a reading program, and hence the first principal acted rationally and wisely, high faculty morale and sense of involvement on the part of the community are also advantages to the school and the second principal's decision was also rational. All of this is to say that position authority cannot often be used alone; principals must increasingly rely on their referent or charismatic influence and the influence of their professional expertise in making rational decisions.

Standard decision-making models, helpful to elementary administrators, usually involve a progression of steps: problem identification, information, generation of alternatives, selection from alternatives, implementation, and, finally, evaluation. More complex models include a feedback system at each step, an awareness of the perceptions of the decision maker, and an understanding of the values orientation of the social group involved in the decision.

As logical and natural as these decision-making steps may be, there are many cases where they are not followed in conflict situations. Confronted during the day with on-the-spot problems and inadequate time and resources, elementary principals make unilateral decisions without examining the assumptions involved in the process or the range of possible alternatives. Instead of obtaining information, understanding self-perceptions and considering the values of the social group, principals may behave reactively, relying wholly on intuition and personal experience. This reactive element is understandable; principals do not work in a vacuum. They do not usually establish individual courses of action, let alone general goals and objectives for school improvement and renewal, without pressure from either the internal or the external environment. Decision making simply does not involve only the decision maker. In a real sense, then, decision making becomes contingent on the difficulty or complexity of the problem situation, the principal's position power, and the quality of the principal's relationships with others.

Some administrators choose "safe" or bureaucratic decision-making strategies, proceeding in the same direction and making school policy as they have previously. This kind of decision making may be successful in situations that are already highly favorable to the principal, or even highly unfavorable situations where no possibility of consensus or involvement exists. In intermediate situations, however, the established bureaucratic policies and procedures may be ineffective since the problems are both more complex and less clearly defined.

Principals who are not responsive to these intermediate problem situations continue to support, or to rely on, previous policy, hoping that time will take care of the problem; they may also delay decision making until they are certain of acceptance of their decisions. In these ways, principals continue to operate on the institutional dimension of the social system of the school while ignoring the individual dimension. In the language of situational leadership theory, such principals are quite likely to be low in both "task orientation" and "relations orientation." They have little interest in completing a task, such as developing a revised curriculum in mathematics, and show, in general, a disinterest in "getting the job done." They also show little concern for cooperative and harmonious relationships with others in the school. The key element here of this bureaucratic style is that it is "separated" from both the task element and the relations element. Such principals, then, practice a separated style of leadership, regardless of the situational realities around them.

Another problem in decision making which elementary school principals face is the problem of incomplete information. There are environmental restraints on how much information is available but furthermore, as psychologists inform us, our short-term memory can apparently retain only a certain number of information items at any one time. If we have more information than we can cope with, we need help. Computers, though readily available, are impractical in most conflict situations, especially where qualitative, rather than quantitative, information needs to be processed. Most elementary school decisions do not lend themselves to computerized management information systems. Thus principals make decisions with incomplete data, limited memory capacity, and partial knowledge of possible alternatives and their consequences.

Elementary principals, then, tend to use rules of thumb, common sense, and heuristics to reduce a complex problem situation into a simpler, more manageable, one. Policies, rules and regulations, and other criteria are also employed in this process. A typical administrator response to a question about a decision that turned out badly is: "With the available information, the choices open to me, and the resources at the time, the choice made was, in my judgment, the best."

PURPOSE OF THIS BOOK

This book is intended to help students of elementary school administration make better decisions and manage conflict or problem situations more successfully by presenting an overview of conflict management and by providing a series of experiences for student practice in conflict management.

The first section of this book sets forth basic concepts of decision making based on current theory, research, and practice in conflict management. These chapters are not intended to be definitive or detailed discussions, and readers are encouraged to peruse the post-chapter references for more complete treatments of related theory and research.

The second section of this book provides vignettes and case studies, giving students of elementary school administration an opportunity to develop both cognitive and group process skills in decision making. The authors have found role playing useful in testing alternative solutions to problem situations. Although time consuming, role playing provides excellent practice for students in developing interpersonal skills and "suffering" the consequences of decisions made.

Introductory questions to the vignette/case study chapters provide some initial direction for coming to grips with the problems involved. The discussion questions after each vignette/case provide specific guidance for dealing with the problems. The authors have found that four general questions can successfully guide the discussion of each vignette/case study, and students are asked to keep them always in mind:

What is the problem?

What are the immediate steps to solving the problem?

What are the long-range steps to solving the problem?

What are the educational policy implications of the solutions recommended?

This book is designed to be of interest and use to the novice as well as the seasoned administrator and should be an especially helpful resource for educators studying to be elementary school principals. As stated at the outset, it is the authors' hope that conflict will not be regarded as always detrimental to the school but, when properly understood, often provides opportunities for decision making which can improve the school and advance its educational purposes.

This new edition includes several changes. As part of the Introduction, the authors have included a discussion on analyzing the vignettes using a sample vignette. The authors have expanded the discussion of decision making to include decision styles in Chapter II. A discussion of site-based management and human resources has been added to Chapter III. Also, a brief discussion on adapting the vignettes and cases to the secondary school level concludes Chapter III. A subject index has been developed for this edition as well. Finally, the authors have supplemented the original set of vignettes with ten new ones reflecting recent problems faced by elementary schools and their principals.

ANALYZING A VIGNETTE OR CASE

After reading the vignette, **José Wants to Go to the Circus,** page 111, the reader will recognize that the principal is going to be involved in a conflict situation and will need to meet with the disputants: the teacher and the parent. Part of the process in resolving this conflict situation is preparing for a confrontation. That is, to think about your resources, to think creatively, and to see if you can adopt a positive manner in relating to the parental problem.

To reach a proper settlement or solution to this problem a positive climate must be achieved. This requires that the principal avoid a power struggle; that both he, the teacher, and the parent consider José's education as a high stake enterprise; that he can work with José's parent; and that he can engage in joint problem solving.

Power is seductive to most people. It enables the powerful to wield influence or dominate. In this vignette the principal needs to avoid this seduction. In this conflict situation the principal can be a winner, a loser, or can avoid the power problem and focus on solving the problem. When the focus is on problem solving both sides can be in a win/win situation.

Before meeting with the parent or any other person in a confrontation it is necessary to get the facts. Facts in a confrontation situation are situated in the context of a person's perception and need to be understood from that vantage point. The coordinator states that José is a very active child. He has difficulty following directions and tends to lash out at people near him for no apparent reason. He would be a danger to himself and other children on a field trip. She feels that he would need an adult to individually supervise him during the whole field trip. After discussing the problem with the teacher, the principal then begins to think about the problem.

Principals in most instances do not want a school problem to be resolved beyond the confines of the school community. In this situation, the parent states she will take the problem to the parent teacher organization, an alderman, and a lawyer. This places some pressure on the principal to negotiate with the parent.

The principal then needs to determine the problem. It can be stated in several ways with different degrees of generality. What should the principal do (1) about a disgruntled parent? (2) about a teacher who refuses to take José on a trip? (3) to best enhance José's educational development? The principal has one other factor to consider when resolving this problem. He must consider the trade off costs for the other children, faculty, and parents. However, by focusing on José's educational development the teacher, parent, and principal start with the same problem. This minimizes the baggage of power, authority, and domination and identifies the purpose of the negotiations.

Another factor that must be considered in conflict management is for the principal to estimate what he would like to happen and what he could accept. In other words what is the principal's bottom line. The principal might say to himself, "I would like to keep things as they are. I could accept José going on the trip if I could be sure he wouldn't interfere with the teacher and the other students' learning and that he could be removed at any time if he did. But in any case, under no circumstances can I let a child who can be a danger to himself or another child go on this trip without excellent supervision."

The parent has as her purpose to get the coordinator to take José, and the coordinator's purpose is to exclude José from the trip. Both had a different problem with different solutions. The principal's intent is to enhance José's educational development. After asking each participant to state her position, the principal visualizes the purpose as the identification of the problem and how a solution will preserve an effective school policy. The principal does not attempt to solve the problem as posed by the other participants, but he does have some estimate of his bottom line. It is also necessary to be specific when asked the meaning of the broader idea used to encompass the interests of both parties. It does no good to obfuscate the conflict by saying that by educational enhancement you mean to increase José's reading scores in the context of the present issue.

In managing conflict, the interests of the parties need to be considered. In a school organization the principal should build a school culture for all members of the school community that has meaning, provides some feeling of autonomy, and encourages people to feel effective. The school culture should encourage the members to accept the idea that behavior shapes attitudes not vice versa. When decisions are made in consideration of the parties' interests and the mission statement of the school, the quality of the decisions will maintain the integrity of the organization.

The next step in resolving this problem is to consider all the possible alternatives. These should be formed before the meeting. However, during the meeting other alternatives may be offered that are acceptable. Some alternatives the principal could have developed before the meeting were as follows:

1) Ask for another opinion from the counselor or school psychologist.
2) Ask the teacher to let José go. Perhaps she is too inflexible.
3) Tell the parent José cannot go. José would be a spoiler and a danger to the trip.
4) Let José go providing the mother or father or another responsible adult accompanies José on the trip and takes responsibility for the supervision of José. If José manifests unacceptable behavior the chaperone will take José home.

If the principal decided that his best option was the last, he would be supportive of the teacher and coordinator and still allow José to go on the trip. This, he hoped, would satisfy the parent and the teacher.

Another factor that needs to be considered is whether to bring both parties together to resolve a problem or to deal with the parties separately. This decision can be difficult to estimate. It seems reasonable to ask the teacher if she would like to meet with the parent and the principal to deal with this conflict. Here it appears that at least the teacher has not come to an emotional impasse and can deal with the parent in a face-to-face meeting. If the two parties have already "come to blows" it makes more sense to hear both sides of the conflict and talk with each party individually.

While discussing the problem the principal asks both disputants what they can recommend to resolve the conflict. If they do not recommend a possible solution the principal states his best option. He alleviates the teacher's concern about José's behavior and enables the parent to get her need satisfied.

The decision in this vignette can be identified as transactional. According to the Getzels-Guba social systems model (Getzels, Lipham, and Campbell, 1968), a transactional decision is one that can strengthen both the organization and the participant. The teacher and school's policy concerning field trips is supported and the parent is given the opportunity to have José go on the field trip. In most confrontation situations there are usually long-range solutions, modifications of policy, or changes in procedures that need to be established to avoid similar confrontations from occurring in the future. In the present case, the principal can discuss the requirements for field trip participation. He then might put into the parent handbook a paragraph explaining the requirements for students going on a field trip and that teachers should inform parents about their particular field trip requirements.

Most of the vignettes in this book deal with conflict between two or more persons. The same principles in these vignettes usually can be applied to conflict between groups (e.g., unions and administration, teachers and teachers, parents and parents).

REFERENCES

Nelson F. Dubois, George F. Alverson, and Richard K. Staley, **Educational Psychology and Instructional Decisions** (Homewood, Illinois: The Dorsey Press, 1979).

Fred E. Fiedler, **A Theory of Leadership Effectiveness** (New York: McGraw-Hill, 1967).

Jacob W. Getzels, James M. Lipham, and Ronald F. Campbell, **Educational Administration As A Social Process: Theory, Research, Practice** (New York: Harper and Row, 1968).

Richard A. Gorton, **Leadership and School Administration: Important Concepts, Case Studies, and Simulations,** 3rd edition (Dubuque, Iowa: William C. Brown, 1987).

Emil J. Haller and Kenneth A. Strike, **An Introduction to Educational Administration** (White Plains, NY: Longman, Inc., 1986).

A. Henry Lauchland, **The Professional's Guide to Working Smarter** (Tenafly, NJ: Burrill-Ellsworth Associates, 1988).

Harry Levinson, ed., **Designing and Managing Your Career: Advice from the Harvard Business Review** (Boston: Harvard Business School Press, 1988).

James M. Lipham, **The Principalship: Foundations and Functions** (New York: Harper and Row, 1974).

W. J. Reddin, **Managerial Effectiveness** (New York: McGraw-Hill, 1970).

Thomas J. Sergiovanni and David Elliott, **Educational and Organizational Leadership in Elementary Schools** (Englewood Cliffs, New Jersey: Prentice-Hall, 1975).

Stuart C. Smith and Philip K. Piele, eds., **School Leadership: Handbook for Excellence,** 2nd ed. (Eugene, OR: ERIC Clearing House on Educational Management, 1989).

Karolyn J. Snyder and Robert H. Anderson, **Managing Productive Schools: Toward an Ecology** (San Diego: Harcourt Brace Jovanovich, Inc., 1986).

BASIC CONFLICT AND
DECISION-MAKING CONCEPTS

1

Conflict and Its Management

Change occurs in our society with increasing rapidity. Technological innovations, economic restructurings, new laws, political forces, and the media, as examples, all engender change in American society and, consequently, American education. The elementary school responds, as do other educational institutions, by integrating the compatible changes into the school organization, but it is seldom a problem-free process. Conflicts often occur during a period of adaptation to social or educational change.

Neither this book nor common sense suggests that we should learn to suppress change or the conflict which it may cause in our educational institutions. Properly managed, many conflicts are catalysts for improving the efficiency and effectiveness of the school. But in order to achieve this effectiveness, elementary school principals need to learn how to identify conflict and how to manage it appropriately; they need to be aware of the types of conflicts and the positive approaches for resolution. For our purposes here, we can separate conflict into five categories: intrapersonal, interpersonal, intragroup, intergroup, and intraorganizational.

INTRAPERSONAL CONFLICT

Intrapersonal conflict occurs within the self and emerges because the individual has difficulty in choosing personal goals. Three types of intrapersonal conflict can be identified as occurring when there is a choice (1) between two positive outcomes, (2) between a positive and negative outcome, and (3) between two negative outcomes. A choice between two positive outcomes, while presenting some difficulty in deciding, does not usually cause conflict, and a choice between a negative and positive outcome is normally easy. Difficulty arises, however, when the choice is between two negative outcomes and intrapersonal conflict may result.

Another source of intrapersonal conflict is cognitive dissonance, the holding of two incompatible beliefs. In this state the individual becomes psychologically uncomfortable and is motivated to achieve a new state of cognitive equilibrium, or consonance, by either obtaining more information or by changing a belief. If one has spent considerable effort in reducing dissonance and then finds that the end result was not sound, one tends to justify the decision rather than admit error. Students of elementary school administration should be particularly aware of this intrapersonal dynamic. If a principal does not admit error in such a situation, human and material resources in the school could be committed to a bad choice.

INTERPERSONAL CONFLICT

Interpersonal conflict commonly involves two parties, although, in school situations, it is possible to have several groups in conflict. Principals may often have to consider teachers, students, and parents in particular conflicts. The principles for dealing with such conflict remain the same but the addition of interested parties may make the problem more complex.

Thomas presents five administrative styles for dealing with interpersonal, or organizational, conflict (see Figure 1.1). The elementary principal should be in a position to choose among and use the appropriate styles of management when faced with interpersonal conflict.

The five styles shown here are based on two interrelated factors: assertion and cooperation. The desire to satisfy one's own concerns (assertion) and to satisfy the concerns of others (cooperation) constitute the vertical and horizontal axes of the model in Figure 1.1. Thus, to "avoid" conflict is represented at the lower ends of each axis; to avoid conflict is both unassertive and uncooperative. Principals showing such behavior tend to isolate themselves in their offices, remaining neutral and seeking to avoid conflict. Although this may seem to be only "unassertive" it is also uncooperative; teachers, for example, would become frustrated with such behavior and view it unfavorably.

FIGURE   1.1   Conflict-Handling Styles

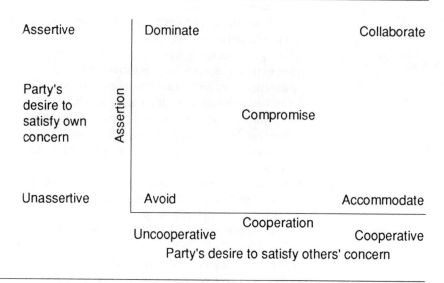

Adapted from Kenneth W. Thomas, "Conflict and Conflict Management" in Marvin D. Dunnette, Editor, **Handbook of Industrial and Organizational Psychology.** Copyright © 1976 by Rand McNally College Publishing Company. Reprinted by permission by John Wiley and Sons, Inc.

On the other hand, principals who use dominating behavior, high on the vertical axis, try to reach predetermined goals without respect for the interest of others. They may decide that to "win" while others "lose" is the only means to an end, but teachers would assess such assertive but uncooperative behavior unfavorably. It should be noted that assertive behavior may sometimes be effective; if the goals of teachers and parents are congruent with those of the principal, fewer conflicts may arise and the principal's assertive behavior may more likely be tolerated. Effectiveness of this assertive style is dependent upon congruities between the participants in a conflict.

A third style of interpersonal conflict management is "accommodative," high in cooperative behavior and low in assertive behavior. Principals using this style may be trying to assume an altruistic posture by accepting both reasonable and unreasonable requests from teachers and parents, but such a posture abandons leader responsibility and may seriously reduce the effectiveness of the school in reaching its goals. Even though, with the accommodative style, the frequency of conflicts may well be reduced and principals apparently assessed in a favorable light by their teachers and parents, these principals might also be seen as weak.

The fourth category, "compromise," is the result of a balance between assertion and cooperation to "split the difference" in resolving a conflict which results in partial satisfaction—and partial dissatisfaction—to the disputing parties. The most obvious example of compromise, both as a strategy and an outcome, can be seen in such conflicts as collective negotiations. When an impasse occurs during such a process, mediators, fact finders, and ultimately arbitrators are called in to assist the parties in a compromise settlement in which neither party's interests are harmed too severely and each party can save face. This collective negotiations model has become popular enough in the literature on conflict that the term "negotiations" itself is a crucial variable in a number of problem-solving approaches to conflict resolution. The principal as compromiser may often be viewed favorably by the parties to a conflict, but the compromise solution may also be viewed as a short-term solution; a series of compromises may be a series of short-term solutions. Favorable assessment of the principal for the compromised short-term solution may dissipate rapidly if a long-term solution is not forthcoming.

Long-term solutions to conflict situations are the goal of the fifth category, the collaborative style. This style is represented at the upper right of the figure, at the highest levels of both cooperative and assertive behaviors. The collaborative style is characterized by trust, candidness, and an understanding of different points of view. Conflict is considered natural in such "human" organizations as schools, and no one is sacrificed by "win/lose" decisions. Collaborative principals turn conflict into problem-solving exercises involving all the parties to the dispute, and they tend to be assessed favorably by those parties, especially over a period of time. If principals use the negotiations model as a problem-solving strategy, counter proposals or counter solutions to the conflict will inevitably be formed by the parties under their principal's guidance. Such counter proposals may lead to a compromise solution of some kind, but the important goal that collaborative principals wish the disputing parties to attain is an understanding **and** acceptance of the merits of each party's views on the issue. Communication between the parties is thus enhanced and a long-term solution to the conflict is a better possibility.

INTRAGROUP CONFLICT

On any elementary school faculty, teachers will be divided into different formal and informal groupings such as union and non-union, ethnic majority and minority, traditional and progressive. When issues arise in the school, teachers take sides based in part on their formal or informal group memberships. When intragroup conflict over an issue occurs, the elementary school principal should assess whether its basis is primarily intellectual (substantive) or emotional (affective). Table 1.1 summarizes the elements of conflict resolution within

T A B L E 1.1   Conflict Resolution within Groups

Type of Conflict Resolved	Elements of Group Processes Associated with Successful Conflict Resolution within Groups
Substantive only	1. Group members had facts and used them.
	2. The chairperson sought information from the group and practiced much solution proposing of the agenda items.
	3. Group members suggest solutions and accept each other.
Affective only	1. Group considered problems independent of each other.
	2. Frequently postponed items that were difficult.
	3. Group members withdrew from interpersonal contact.
Substantive and Affective	1. Group expressed a low frequency of personal and self-oriented needs.
	2. A pleasant affective atmosphere was related with a need for unified action.
	3. The problem solving proceeded in an orderly and sequential manner, and all members understood the group vocabulary.
	4. There was a "willingness to give and take."

Adapted from Harold Guetzkow and John Gyr, "An Analysis of Conflict in Decision-Making Groups," **Human Relations** 7, No. 3 (1954): 367–81.

groups regarding the substantive or affective basis of the conflict, for the processes differ dramatically according to the type of conflict involved. The resolution of a substantive conflict requires that group members associate with each other and immerse themselves in the content of the problem. For the resolution of an affective conflict, however, members are best kept independent of each other and not immersed in the problem. In a conflict which has both a substantive and an affective basis, the successful conflict resolution strategy entails a single-minded focus by group members on agreed-upon school needs, one issue at a time.

INTERGROUP CONFLICT

The elementary school principal may be faced minimally with situations that involve intergroup conflict. Team-teaching, age-grouped unit planning, sports activities, and contests between classes in the school, as examples, are situations where intergroup conflict can occur. When classes or homerooms compete against each other for best attendance, most parents belonging to the local parent-teacher organization or the "quietest" class in school, each competing group tends to become more cohesive within itself but also tends to regard itself as superior to the other groups. Hostile attitudes may thus develop between members of the competing groups. As the competition develops, defeatism may occur among members of the less successful groups and formal teaching-learning activities may become subordinated to the excitement of the competition. The approaches to interpersonal conflict resolution discussed previously will aid the elementary school principal in controlling conflict caused by intended and unintended competitive situations.

INTRAORGANIZATIONAL CONFLICT

Although intraorganizational conflict has many faces, it appears to fall, with some overlap, into four categories: (1) vertical, (2) horizontal, (3) line-staff, and (4) role conflict. Vertical conflict is a problem within the hierarchical structure of authority in the school. Principals usually send directives to the teachers by way of written memos or bulletins, a top-down approach to communication. If a policy or rule is perceived by teachers as an infringement upon their interests, a vertical conflict may well ensue between principal and teachers.

Horizontal conflict occurs across the ranks of teachers. Although teachers may be assumed to have similar educational goals, there are many specific categories; special education teachers, counselors, bilingual teachers, regular education teachers and other pupil personnel specialists all have varying educational viewpoints, experiences, and training backgrounds. When these personnel are made more interdependent—as a result, for example, of multi-disciplinary teaming, case study, and individualized education mandates—the possibility of conflict regarding goals and values between these groups increases. Elementary schools with extremely structured rules for pupil promotion that include extensive accountability for student achievement across the ranks of teachers may also experience high incidences of horizontal conflict among the professional staff.

The third type of intraorganizational conflict, line-staff, occurs between the elementary principal and central office personnel. The central office staff controls most material resources as well as performance and program evaluation procedures, and it reflects district-wide rather than individual school points of view. Central office personnel may often have very specialized expertise in educational matters, and the elementary principal needs their support and enthusiasm for any extensive improvements or innovations within the school. Sometimes, however, the central office may issue regulations and procedures or demand reports that particular principals perceive to be irrelevant to the school's needs or interests. Indeed, some principals may view the central office as an adversary who continually infringes on their position authority and power.

Role conflict is an important category in intraorganizational problems although it can be present in other areas of conflict as well. It is considered here as an intraorganizational problem because of the important part which communication between principal and teachers plays. Inherent in all communications are expectations, perceptions, and evaluations or judgments. A principal's message, for example, may be incompatible with, or exert unwarranted pressure on, a teacher's role expectations, perceptions, or judgments. The teacher may then send a message back which either clarifies or further muddles the role conflict. Communication, an important solution for problems, could complicate the problem.

One way out of this communication/role conflict problem is the utilization of informal communication. If principals understand and accept informal communication, via the school's grapevine, as a legitimate way in which professional staff respond to messages, they will be able, in turn, to utilize it—through, for example, the school secretary, a veteran or head teacher, a union representative—in order to get their original message across to the faculty. If principals do not understand or utilize the school's communication grapevine, however, they may perceive individual return messages as insubordination, a challenge to their authority or downright sabotage of the school's programs and goals. If they believe that these return messages, whatever form they take, are incompatible with their role as educational leader of the school, role conflict may be the result.

Role conflict may also occur if there is inadequate or inconsistent information about the requirements of a position in the school. If roles are not well clarified, elementary principals subject themselves to unnecessary crisis management situations and stress. Aggressiveness, hostile communications, and withdrawal may arise in response to unresolved role ambiguity. Such dysfunctional coping techniques may be replaced by joint problem solving, but the conflict need not arise in the first place if principals define, clarify, and communicate their role and its subparts to the faculty. The development and distribution of written position specifications, descriptions, and organizational charts represent more formal ways to resolve potential or real role ambiguity.

ORGANIZATIONAL DILEMMAS

Three potential sources of conflict in the very organization of the school itself are becoming increasingly important and may manifest themselves in interpersonal, intragroup, intergroup, or intraorganizational problems. All three concern the relationships between administrators and teachers in a changing professional situation.

The professional/bureaucratic dilemma is one such source of conflict. Contemporary organizations, including schools, are experiencing both increased professionalization and increased bureaucratization. As might be expected, school administrators tend to hold bureaucratic expectations and teachers tend to hold professional expectations; this dichotomy has a clear potential for conflict situations.

The ability/authority dilemma occurs in situations where the right to make decisions is balanced against having the knowledge and ability to do so. Such conflict may be seen in the formal negotiations process when teachers attempt to win larger areas of decision making and administrators resist what they view as the erosion of their authority.

The autonomy/coordination dilemma is the third source of conflict. As teachers become more professionalized and gain more control over decisions, they tend to become more autonomous. At the same time, the organizational need is for more cooperation and coordination. Again, the stage is set for possible conflict. Autonomous professionals do not always sense the need for coordination, and some do not function well that way. The administrator may have to make special efforts to enlist the cooperation and, in some instances, manage coordination with minimal cooperation from some key persons.

CONFLICT MANAGEMENT: BEYOND AUTHORITY

In all types of conflict discussed here, the school administrator has some type of authority. A principal will often have the delegated, and sometimes statutory, authority that enables him or her to issue formal directives which teachers follow and which help to reduce role ambiguity. Often this position authority is intermediary; the principal merely passes along and enforces a policy or rule dictated by the central office or school board. It may also be possible for the principal to use position authority to settle conflicts among and between parents, teachers, and students. However, when the elementary principal is capable of augmenting position authority with referent and expert power and influence, he or she stands an even better chance of managing conflict in the school.

There are three important methods that an administrator can use to resolve or manage conflict without resorting purely to position authority; the "linking pin" method, the confrontation method and the "neutral party" method. All three involve the blending of position authority with referent authority and influence.

The "linking pin" concept is a structural approach to managing conflict through prevention. The "linking pin" occupies an intermediary position within the organizational structure; it could be a teacher who represents other teachers in the school or is a member of the principal's advisory council. The person who functions in this "linking pin" position utilizes informal communications via the grapevine to pass necessary information to and from principal and staff. Since the "linking pin" approach involves both vertical and horizontal communications, it can help prevent excessive conflict.

The confrontation method can be employed when attempts to manage conflict by structural means will be ineffective or dysfunctional. Although the word "confrontation" may have negative connotations of a win/lose situation in popular parlance, confrontation is essentially a process. The parties to a dispute openly exchange information, directly engage each other in face-to-face relationships and attempt to resolve their differences by reaching an agreed upon outcome. If confrontation is entered into as a win/win situation, the parties to the conflict all gain, a method similar to the collaborative style or strategy previously discussed. On the other hand, if confrontation is perceived as a win/lose situation, the parties will exert force against each other in order to gain at the other's expense.

The third concept of conflict management presented here is the use of the elementary principal as a neutral party. This can occur when the parties involved in conflict believe that the outcomes of a negotiating process will be enhanced by the principal's participation. Negotiations, whether formal or informal, can be considered a process in which each party determines what it must gain and what it can reasonably give up in a transaction. If either party to the negotiations adopts a win/lose posture, the confrontation procedure will probably fail. Table 1.2 indicates some procedural differences between the win/win and win/lose strategies.

As a neutral third party, the elementary principal should adopt win/win procedures in an effort to get the parties to do the same. Furthermore, the principal should determine if the conflict is substantive or affective. (See Table 1.1 in earlier discussion). Substantive conflict usually requires a problem-solving or task-oriented approach while affective conflict requires the principal to apply a relations-oriented approach that emphasizes the maintenance of group members. Impasses, of course, must be broken by the principal acting as a third party, and win/win procedures that interrupt win/lose behaviors can be applied by the principal at the appropriate time.

TABLE 1.2   Negotiations Strategy

Win/Win Strategy	Win/Lose Strategy
1. Define the conflict.	1. Define conflict as a win/lose situation.
2. Pursue common goals.	2. Pursue personal goals.
3. Search for creative agreements that are acceptable to both parties.	3. Force the other party into submission.
4. Emphasize mutual inter-dependence to equalize power.	4. Emphasize one's own independence and the other's dependence to increase one's own power.
5. Use honest, accurate, and open communication of one's proposals, positions, and needs.	5. Use inaccurate, deceitful, and misleading communication of one's proposals, positions, and needs.
6. Avoid threats to reduce the other's defensiveness.	6. Use threats to force submission.
7. Help problem solving by showing flexibility of position.	7. Communicate rigidly regarding one's position.

Adapted from David W. Johnson and Frank P. Johnson, **Joining Together: Group Therapy and Group Skills** (Englewood Cliffs, N.J.: Prentice-Hall Inc., 1975), pp. 182–83.

As a neutral third party, the elementary principal must be trusted and accepted by the conflicting parties in order to provide emotional support. Steps similar to those listed below should be taken by the principal in order to facilitate this trust and acceptance:

1. Encourage the parties to develop incentives for resolving the conflict.
2. Achieve a balance of power between the parties.
3. Coordinate mutually positive responses by the parties to their respective proposals.
4. Encourage openness, provide reassurance and increase trust between the parties.
5. Reduce threat and tension levels so that information and creative alternatives can emerge from the parties.

Confrontation approaches, even involving the principal as a neutral third party, do not assure conflict resolution. But they do provide a means for the parties to begin exploring the nature of their differences. From there an understanding of some of the merits of the other side's position may evolve and, from that understanding, possible solutions involving compromise or win/win strategies may present themselves. There may be times, of course, when the principal simply cannot assume the role of a neutral third party. A student's due process rights, for example, may require the principal to be nonsupportive of a teacher who wants to exclude a student from class because teacher and student do not get along. In appropriate situations, however, the elementary principal may function successfully as a neutral third party and become the catalyst for the eventual resolution of the conflict situation.

The types of conflict and the methods of conflict management explored in this chapter have direct bearing on the elementary administrator's effectiveness as an educational leader. He or she must work on the assumption that conflict is natural and need not have long-term negative consequences for the school. Properly understood and acted upon, conflict management can be the basis upon which people are integrated into the school, and the school becomes a better place to work and learn.

REFERENCES

Chester Barnard, **The Functions of the Executive** (Cambridge: Harvard University Press, 1938).

Robert R. Blake, et al., **Managing Intergroup Conflict in Industry** (Houston: Gulf Publishing Co., 1964).

Ronald Corwin, "Professional Persons in Public Organizations," **Educational Administration Quarterly** 1 (Autumn, 1965): 1–23.

Terrence E. Deal and Lynn D. Celotti, "How Much Influence Do (and Can) Educational Administrators Have on Classrooms?" **Phi Delta Kappan,** March 1980, pp. 471–73.

Allan C. Filley, **Interpersonal Conflict Resolution** (Dallas: Scott, Foresman & Co., 1975).

Roger Fisher and William L. Ury, **Getting to Yes: Negotiating Agreement without Giving In** (New York: Penguin Books, 1983).

John R. P. French and Bertram Raven, "The Basis of Social Power," **Studies in Social Power,** ed. Darwin Cartwright (Ann Arbor: University of Michigan, 1959).

H. Guetzkow and J. Gyr, "An Analysis of Conflict in Decision-Making Groups," **Human Relations** 7 (1954): 367–81.

Daniel J. Isenberg, "Thinking and Managing: A Verbal Protocol Analysis of Managerial Problem Solving," **Academy of Management Journal** 29, No. 4 (December, 1986): 775–788.

David W. Johnson and Frank P. Johnson, **Joining Together: Group Theory and Group Skills,** 3rd ed. (Englewood Cliffs, N.J.: Prentice-Hall, 1987).

Rensis Likert, **New Patterns of Management** (New York: McGraw-Hill Book Co., Inc., 1961).

Rensis Likert and Jane G. Likert, **New Ways of Managing Conflict** (New York: McGraw-Hill, 1976).

Dan C. Lortie, "Built-In Tendencies Toward Stabilizing the Principal's Role," **Journal of Research and Development in Education** 22 (Fall, 1988): 80–90.

Joseph H. McGivney and James M. Haught, "The Politics of Education: A View from the Perspective of the Central Office Staff," **Educational Administration Quarterly** 8 (Autumn, 1972): 18–38.

Alice G. Sargent and Ronald J. Stupak, "Managing in the '90s: The Androgynous Manager," **Training and Development Journal** 43 (December, 1989): 29–35.

Thomas J. Sergiovanni and Robert J. Starratt, **Supervision: Human Perspectives,** 3rd ed. (New York: McGraw-Hill Book Co., 1983).

Dennis P. Slevin, **The Whole Manager: How to Increase Your Professional and Personal Effectiveness** (New York: AMACOM, 1989).

Stuart C. Smith, Diana Ball, and Demetri Liontos, **Working Together: The Collaborative Style of Bargaining,** (Eugene, OR: ERIC Clearing House on Educational Management, 1990).

Phyllis O. Tate, "An Analysis of the Behaviors of Elementary Principals Toward Informal Communication Systems" (unpublished Ph.D. dissertation, Loyola University of Chicago, 1982.).

K. W. Thomas, "Conflict and Conflict Management," **Handbook of Industrial and Organizational Psychology,** ed. Marvin D. Dunnette (Chicago: Rand McNally College Publishing Co., 1976), pp. 889–936.

CHAPTER

2

Decision Making and Conflict Management

There are a number of factors that limit rational decision making by the elementary principal. Although only a limited amount of information can be processed at one time, the principal must be careful to avoid simplifying complex problems by ignoring relevant data. The habitual simplification of problem situations results in the "don't confuse me with facts" syndrome. Habitual simplification of problems may lead to inappropriate or incomplete solutions which cause the principal to continually consume even more time and resources. The principal will then wonder why all the attention and effort have not paid off.

Problem simplification can lead to obstructionist shortcuts called "decision-making traps." These traps may be classified into the errors of representativeness, availability, and adjustment/anchoring (Tversky and Kahneman 1974). All elementary principals are susceptible to these perception traps. When the principals opt to maximize gains and minimize losses, they may, in turn, exhibit behavior—decision-making traps—that obstructs their perception of available evidence. The autocratic principal may be more susceptible to the traps than the participatory principal.

Representativeness is the behavior strategy that an elementary principal sometimes uses when confronted with a new problem situation. The principal attempts to substitute stereotypes in an effort to cope with the situation. For example, the teacher of a recently transferred fifth grade pupil who is well groomed, well spoken, friendly, and good looking, and whose father is a college professor, indicates the pupil earned a perfect score on a medium difficulty math test. The combination of the perfect score with the accompanying stereotypes of "success" may cause the pupil to be viewed as above average in ability or intelligence. In this scenario, the frequency of events, such as scores on a number of math tests taken over time, is not considered. A conclusion of high ability or brilliance on the basis of a single observation is unreliable and prediction would be hazardous as to the pupil's future achievement. In this case, the accompanying stereotypes caused the math score to be taken as representative of the student's ability. To assume the representativeness of an isolated act will obstruct rational decision making.

Mistaken conclusions regarding the probable frequency of an event can result from the elementary principal's use of another available, but incorrect, strategy: the "availability" of data. If an event is remembered vividly, or of recent occurrence, or frequently repeated, one will be more likely to recall it. If a previously disruptive pupil and an unusually quiet and well-mannered pupil are sent to the school's office for fighting, the principal will have a rather strong tendency to think that the pupil with the history of disruptive behavior is at fault. The nature and prevalence of the disruptive pupil's past conduct are "available" to the decision maker who may decide guilt or innocence on the basis of past behavior. To the busy elementary principal, the availability strategy, though it may lead to incorrect decisions, is "easy" and, therefore, likely to be used.

Adjustment/anchoring is a third strategy which may hinder rational decision making. The elementary principal often maintains some consistency between an initial conclusion and subsequent evidence related to the conclusion. Care should be taken to avoid interpreting data on the basis of that original perception, however. Over a period of time, for example, a consistently disruptive pupil is observed less frequently in altercations with other pupils. However, because of the pupil's previous aggressive conduct, the elementary principal may still perceive the pupil as being more aggressive than the evidence now indicates. Hence, the principal's use of adjustment/anchoring to hold to an earlier conclusion despite new evidence to the contrary can contribute to dysfunctional decision making.

Principals who administer their schools with an autocratic or authoritarian leadership style usually make decisions unilaterally. Therefore, they may find themselves in the unenviable position of making more serious decision errors than participatory principals. A principal may have made a decision with a high level of personal confidence, but the decision may not be viewed as satisfactory by the teachers, other staff, parents, and students. The elementary principal, then, is well advised to utilize a collaborative decision-making model where a complex problem situation exists that directly affects one or more of the significant groups committed to the school. Where a problem situation is of little or no concern to one or more of the school's significant interest groups or an emergency exists, the principal's decision making usually results in a consensus quickly. Other groups will realize that either only one decision was possible (i.e., evacuate the building in case of a fire) or the decision was viewed as one the principal should make (i.e., determine when inclement weather will keep pupils indoors).

DECISION RULES

Since collaborative decision making requires time, the principal should be aware of certain decision rules articulated by Cartwright (1971) typically involved in small group decision-making processes: majority rule, coalition rule, and mean rule. In a faculty meeting, if the majority of teachers favor a position, that position becomes the group's decision. This is the process of majority rule. If 75 percent of a faculty wants to purchase a publisher's reading program, usually the entire faculty then agrees to adopt the program. About 70 percent of all groups that initially obtains a majority on an issue will use majority rule to come to an action decision.

Coalition rule often is attained where a majority view does not exist, but a plurality does occur. A compromise occurs when the 40 percent of the group with the same position persuades another smaller faction composed of another 20 percent that holds a somewhat similar position to form a coalition so an action decision can be made by the whole group. Approximately 80 percent of all groups that obtains a coalition will use coalition rule when there exists no majority position.

Finally, where no favored position exists in a group either by majority or coalition, the groups will usually follow a mean rule. Members of the groups select the position that is approximately the middle position for the whole group. At least 50 percent of all groups faced with no majority or plurality position on an issue will adopt the mean rule so an action decision can be made. Hence, the elementary principal can predict approximately 75 percent of the time the faculty's ultimate position in a situation where the initial position of the faculty is known.

Though a group may come to a compromise decision on an issue, the likelihood that group members will still think their respective initial positions were better is high. A group, therefore, can make an action decision but still experience "foot dragging" among its members while implementing the decision. Where any length of time occurs between the decision and its implementation, the elementary principal should continually express the importance and reasonable-

FIGURE 2.1   Authority-Freedom Continuum

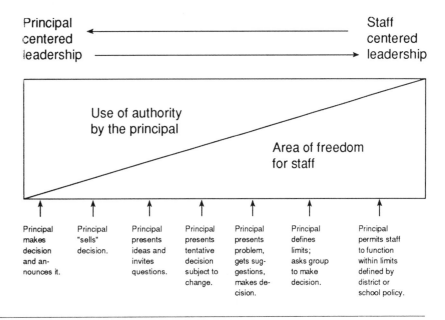

Principal
centered
leadership

Staff
centered
leadership

Use of authority
by the principal

Area of freedom
for staff

| Principal makes decision and announces it. | Principal "sells" decision. | Principal presents ideas and invites questions. | Principal presents tentative decision subject to change. | Principal presents problem, gets suggestions, makes decision. | Principal defines limits; asks group to make decision. | Principal permits staff to function within limits defined by district or school policy. |

ness of the decision to members of the faculty. This high relations-oriented approach to leadership may well eliminate and certainly minimize the problems involved in decision implementation.

By using decision rules to save time, the elementary principal may opt for minimally acceptable positions within the typical school faculty structure. When the range of the faculty's opinion is quickly determined, the elementary principal may surmise which decision rules will be utilized. The principal is then in a position to suggest the appropriate compromise decision to the group. Hence, the elementary principal becomes the efficient facilitator enabling the group to arrive at an acceptable action decision.

THE AUTHORITY-FREEDOM CONTINUUM

A model for decision making that allows the elementary principal to choose decision points along an authority-freedom continuum has been developed by Tannenbaum and Schmidt. Figure 2.1 shows seven decision points along a continuum from which the principal can choose. For the elementary principal, the choice depends on the extent to which the school's significant interest groups should participate in the decision making on any particular issue or problem. The model suggests that different situations require different degrees of involvement by others. The astute elementary principal will remember that when a decision directly affects one or more groups in the school, the participation of group members in the decision making will both facilitate the resolution of the problem or issue and the principal's leadership position in the school.

DECISION STYLES

The elementary principal faces a potential problem in his or her role as decision maker. The principal can make the decision unilaterally or be quite participative. Vroom and Yetton (1973) developed a model of decision making that includes five decision styles. Table 2.1 shows that the decision styles range from autocratic (A1) to consultative (C1) to group consensus (G11).

Later, Vroom and Jago (1988) discussed a decision tree for implementing the five styles. The original model's effectiveness and usefulness in schools has not been established yet. Still, illustration of the different styles of participation in decision making may be useful to the elementary principal.

When principals use consultative and participative styles of leadership there may be both negative and positive effects. The negative effects include the expenditure of time and energy (human capital costs). Teachers and administrators have only so much time and energy to devote to their profession. When dealing with a particular problem, they may not be completing other tasks. The costs of holding a meeting, for example, must be compared with not holding the meeting. The positive features of participative decision making are that teachers and others believe they are members of a team, commitment and loyalty to the decision may be strengthened, and there can be an improvement in staff leadership skills and technical talents.

Similar to the authority-freedom continuum (Figure 2.1), Hoy and Miskel (1990) provided some guidance concerning when to make an autocratic decision or include the staff in a decision. They based their model on two concepts: teacher expertise and relevancy. If the problem to be solved is relevant to the teachers' work and the teachers have expertise to contribute to its solution, the principal should always consult the teachers. If the teachers can only contribute expertise but the problem is not relevant or vice versa, the teachers should rarely be consulted. If the teachers have no expertise to contribute to the problem's solution and the problem is not relevant, the teachers should not be consulted. For example, teachers

TABLE 2.1   Decision Styles for Leading a Group

Leading a Group

A1   You solve the problem or make the decision yourself, using information available to you at the time.

A11   You obtain any necessary information from subordinates, then decide on the solution to the problem yourself. The role played by your subordinate in making the decision is clearly one of providing specific information that you request, rather than generating or evaluating solutions.

C1   You share the problem with relevant subordinates individually, getting their ideas and suggestions without bringing them together as a group. Then you make the decision. This decision may or may not reflect your subordinates' influence.

C11   You share the problem with your subordinates in a group meeting. In this meeting, you obtain their ideas and suggestions. Then you make the decision, which may or may not reflect your subordinates influence.

G11   You share the problem with your subordinates as a group. Together, you generate and evaluate alternatives and attempt to reach a consensus on a solution. Your role is much like that of chairperson, coordinating the discussion, keeping it focused on the problem, and making sure that the critical issues are discussed. You do not try to influence the group to adopt "your" solution, and you are willing to accept and implement any solution that has the support of the entire group.

Source: Vroom, V. H., and Yetton, P. W. *Leadership and Decision Making*. Pittsburgh: University of Pittsburgh Press, 1973, 13.

may have expertise in curriculum and it is relevant to them. Thus, the principal should consult the teachers in curricular matters. Teachers may not have expertise in the purchase of standard cooking equipment for the lunchroom and such equipment is not relevant to their work. They should not be involved in decision making in this area. If the principal does involve them in this type of task, teachers may wonder why the principal has his or her position. The area of concern may be relevant for the teachers (e.g., the organization of the payroll department), but if they have no expertise, they should not be involved. An elementary language arts teacher may have expertise in writing business brochures but the writing of informational brochures for the school district is not relevant to his or her work as a teacher. Therefore, he or she should not be involved in deciding who should write informational brochures for the school district. Thus, there is guidance for the elementary principal in determining when to be autocratic and when to be participative. The degree of participation (Table 2.1. C1, C11, and G11) depends on the situation.

Choosing the appropriate decision-making style can be troublesome for the elementary principal. Currently there is a strongly stated preference for democratic participative decision making in the United States and Japanese business communities. However, participative decision making is not appropriate for all situations as the contingency models indicate (see pages 25–28). The Hoy and Miskel and Vroom and Yetton models make that point as well. Unlike Fiedler's contingency model (see page 26), Vroom and Yetton and Hoy and Miskel, like Hersey and Blanchard (see pages 27–28), assume that leaders can choose from among several leadership styles that reflect the kind of decision to be made.

SOLVING COMPLEX PROBLEMS

Some problem situations are so complex that they defy easy solution. The chances of resolving a particular conflict may vary from very low to highly probable. In some situations, minor progress at any point in time may be a positive step towards solution in the long-term.

A Continuum of Conflict Resolution

Figure 2.2 depicts a continuum of conflict resolution. Any movement from left to right represents progress toward resolution of the conflict situation. When conditions or attitudes among the school's significant interest groups appear predisposed to resolve conflict at the impasse stage, the elementary principal then has the opportunity to intervene toward the right on the continuum. The elementary principal must be alert to any predispositions at the impasse stage so that timing of his or her efforts at conflict resolution will be appropriate.

FIGURE 2.2   Continuum of Conflict Resolution

Conflict Situation Exists	Impasse, no progress	Minor progress	Considerable progress	Important progress	Complete progress	Conflict Situation Resolved

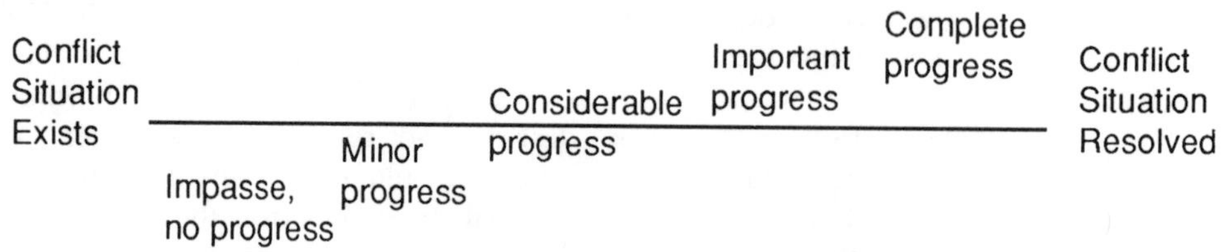

FIGURE 2.3   Model of Decision-Making Process

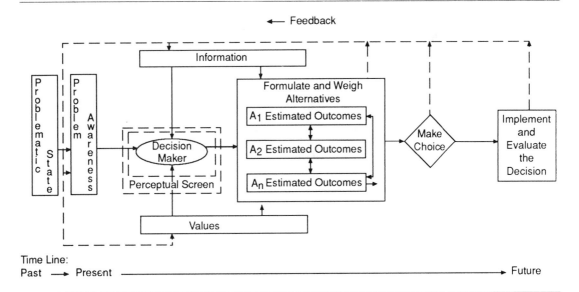

Reprinted by permission of the publisher from Jack A. Culbertson, Curtis Henson, and Ruel Morrison: **Performance Objectives for School Principals** © 1974 by McCutchan Publishing Corporation, Berkeley, California.

Systems Approaches to Decision Making

When faced with a complex problem situation, the elementary principal may be wise to consider a systems approach towards its solution. In utilizing a systems approach, the decision maker realizes a problem situation is composed of at least several interrelated variables. Attention and effort directed toward one variable in the problem situation inevitably affects the other variables. The elementary principal must have a means by which the relevant interrelated variables can be identified and assessed, and alternative outcomes predicted as a result of variable manipulation.

Several systems approaches to decision making have appeared in the educational administration and supervision literature in recent years. Lipham has developed a model that could be useful to the elementary principal. Figure 2.3 shows the interrelated nature of the variables in the decision-making model. Of particular import are the values, perceptual screen, and feedback components of the model. Consideration of these components should aid the elementary principal in understanding the views of significant interest groups, the principal's own dispositions, and the value of each variable in the decision-making process for providing information (feedback) to assist in making subsequent decisions regarding the same or similar problem situations.

FIGURE 2.4   Sequential Steps in Decision Making

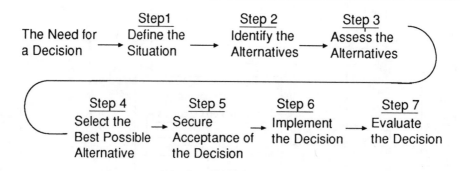

From Gorton, Richard A., **School Administration and Supervision: Important Issues, Concepts, and Case Studies** 2nd ed. © 1972, 1980 Wm. C. Brown Publishers, Dubuque, Iowa. All Rights Reserved. Reprinted by permission.

Decision-making models usually emphasize the necessity and central importance of developing alternative solutions or decisions in problem resolution. Figure 2.3 highlights the importance of alternatives so that the best decision, among the several available, can be selected and implemented. In a more simplified systems model, Gorton urges problem definition, identification and assessment of alternatives, alternative choice, decision approval and implementation, and evaluation. Figure 2.4 shows how each succeeding step is related to a previous step and may only occur if the conditions in the prior step have been essentially fulfilled. Of course, information is necessary at every step but especially in the development of step 2. As in Lipham's model, personal/community values and constraints must be considered throughout the steps of Gorton's model.

A curriculum or academic program decision-making model also can be available to the elementary principal. Marks, Stoops, and King-Stoops have designed a systems approach to curriculum development shown in Figure 2.5. The reader is urged to note the similarities in the interrelated components of this model to those in the two models previously discussed. In this model, the statement of academic objectives precedes the step of generating alternatives central to all the models.

Systems Approaches in Complex Situations

These systems approaches to decision making are merely introduced here to show the reader the availability of conceptual tools or models to aid in the development of solutions to complex problems or conflict situations. These tools are especially useful where time is

FIGURE 2.5   Model of Curriculum Decision Making

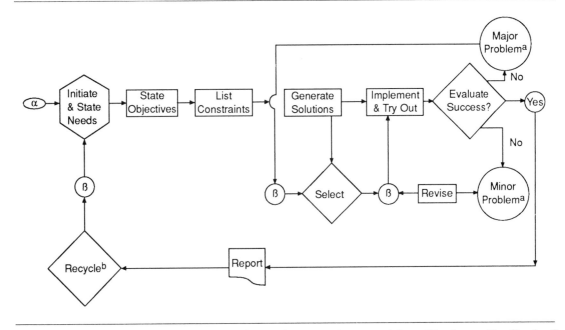

From Sir James Robert Marks, Emery Stoops, and Joyce King-Stoops, **Handbook of Educational Supervision: A Guide for the Practitioner,** Third Edition. Copyright © 1985 by Allyn and Bacon, Inc. Reprinted with permission.

available to the elementary principal to implement the various steps and where long-term solutions are necessary or mandated. In complex problem situations, more than one solution strategy and much group participation usually are required. The school's significant interest groups may well expect the elementary principal to take the needed time and effort to resolve a problem or conflict properly rather than to invoke a temporary "quick fix" solution to save time and effort.

REFERENCES

G. F. Alverson, "An Investigation of the Cognitive-Social Process Underlying Group Induced Shifts," **Dissertation Abstracts International** 37 (1976): 2729A.

D. Cartwright, "Risk Taking by Individuals and Group: An Assessment of Research Employing Chance Dilemmas," **Journal of Personality and Social Psychology** 20 (1971): 361–78.

Sharon C. Conley, "Who's on First? School Reform, Teacher Participation, and the Decision-Making Process," **Education and Urban Society** 21, No. 4 (August, 1984): 366–379.

Andrew E. Dubin, ed., **Principal as Chief Executive Officer** (New York: Falmer Press, 1991).

Michael Fullan, **The New Meaning of Educational Change,** 2nd ed. (New York: Columbia Teachers College, 1991).

Richard A. Gorton, **School Leadership and Administration: Important Concepts, Case Studies, and Simulations,** 3rd ed. (Dubuque, IA.: William C. Brown, 1987).

Wayne K. Hoy and Cecil G. Miskel, **Educational Administration: Theory, Research, and Practice,** 3rd ed. (New York: McGraw-Hill 1990).

Irving L. Janis, **Crucial Decisions: Leadership in Policy Making and Crisis Management** (New York: Free Press, 1988).

Frederick F. Lighthall and Susan D. Allan, **Local Realities, Local Adaptations: Problem, Process, and Person in a School's Governance** (New York, The Falmer Press, 1989).

James M. Lipham, "Improving the Decision-Making Skills of the Principal," Chapter 4 in **Performance Objectives for School Principals: Concepts and Instruments,** eds. Jack A. Culbertson, Curtis Henson, and Ruel Morrison (Berkeley, Calif.: McCutchan, 1974), pp. 83–111.

Sir James R. Marks, Emery Stoops, and Joyce King-Stoops, **Handbook of Educational Supervision: A Guide for the Practitioner,** 3rd ed. (Boston: Allyn and Bacon, Inc., 1985).

Theodore Rubin, **Overcoming Indecisiveness** (New York: Avon Books, 1986).

B. J. Meadows, "The Rewards and Risks of Shared Leadership," **Phi Delta Kappan** '71, No.7 (March, 1990): 545–548.

Robert Tannenbaum and Warren H. Schmidt, "How to Choose a Leadership Pattern," **Harvard Business Review** 36, No. 2 (May–June, 1973).

A. Tversky and D. Kahneman, "Judgment and Uncertainty: Heuristics and Biases," **Science,** Vol. 185, pp. 1124–31.

Charles E. Wales, Anne H. Nardi, and Robert A. Stager, "Decision Making: A New Paradigm for Education," **Educational Leadership** 43, No. 8 (May, 1986): 37–41.

Richard Wynn and Charles W. Guditus, **Team Management: Leadership by Consensus** (Columbus: Charles E. Merrill Publishing Co., 1984).

Victor H. Vroom and Arthur G. Jago, **The New Leadership: Managing Participations in Organizations** (Englewood Cliffs, NJ: Prentice-Hall, 1988).

Victor H. Vroom and Philip W. Yetton, **Leadership and Decision Making** (Pittsburgh: University of Pittsburgh Press, 1973).

3

Contingency and Human Resources Leadership

To conclude these initial chapters, a brief presentation of the contingency approach to elementary school leadership and a discussion of the human resources perspective follow. Often viewed in terms of a leader behavior model, the contingency approach emphasizes the situation in which the elementary principal is placed. The human resources perspective is a response to the more manipulative human relations perspective on the management of people in the workplace. Elementary principals should know the difference between these two perspectives as they develop working relationships with teachers in their schools.

SOME MODELS OF THE CONTINGENCY APPROACH TO LEADERSHIP

According to Morse and Lorsch (1970), the situation is comprised of the task(s) to be performed, the organizational structure, and the kind of people who work in the organization. In the elementary school, some tasks may be highly structured such as the steps by which teachers may order material and supplies for their classrooms or the procedure by which the school secretary checks out student absences. Other tasks may be quite unstructured such as helping a new teacher contend with hostile prejudice in a racially mixed classroom or quieting a delegation of angry parents who want a socially nonconformist teacher fired. For the latter tasks, the elementary principal cannot rely on a pat set of procedures or steps that insure acceptable outcomes.

The elementary school's organizational structure can be flat or hierarchial in terms of formal authority and reporting relationships. It can be a mini-bureaucracy or a professional partnership. The staff in an elementary school is primarily composed of highly educated, child-centered persons concerned with the development of the whole child, each with different motives and needs of teaching and guiding children; and they all will have a need to feel competent in their work.

Organization-task fit, effectiveness of task performance, and the individual's sense of competence are interrelated with resulting implications for management practice. Morse and Lorsch tend to believe that the best possible managerial strategy is to tailor the organization to fit the task and the people. This strategy may be useful for principals as they relate to increasingly experienced teachers engaged in a common educational task.

Elementary school principals, to be successful, must be continually aware of the interacting factors that comprise the situation in which they work. Taking account of one situational factor, such as organization structure, while ignoring or slighting other situational factors could lead to failure in leadership. The elementary principal tries daily to bring about the optimum task-organization-people "fit" possible in the elementary school. The extent to which the principal is able to bring about the optimum "fit" will determine, the contingency approach suggests, the extent to which the principal will be viewed as a successful leader.

Fiedler's now classic model (1969) emphasizes the interaction among leader-member relations, task structure and the leader's position power. The relative strength or weakness among these factors determines a situation in which a leader will be either task- or relations-oriented. According to this version of contingency theory, a person's fundamental leadership style (task- or relation-oriented) is determined by the personality. Therefore, elementary principals should be placed in situations (school settings) that best match their leadership style. Thus Fiedler's theory suggests that attempts to change a principal's personality-anchored leadership style to better fit the school setting will in all likelihood be doomed to failure and result in unsuccessful leadership.

According to Fiedler's theory, the three aforementioned factors or variables are likely to determine whether a given situation will be favorable or unfavorable to the elementary principal. In small group situations, different combinations of leader-member relations (extent to which others will follow a principal because he or she is admired and liked), task structure (extent to which the work is well defined with precisely stated objectives), and the leader's position power (formal authority) suggest the effective leader style: relations-oriented or task-oriented. Where the situations are most favorable (good relations, structured task, and great position power) or least favorable (poor relations, unstructured task, and low position power) to the principal, a task-oriented style is best. In intermediate or mixed situations, a relations-oriented style is best. Arguably, the principal in today's elementary school may be more likely to encounter situations of intermediate favorableness to his or her leadership. Therefore, a person who by nature (personality) is inclined towards getting along with and accommodating others may reflect the appropriate leadership style for success as an elementary school principal.

Still another conceptualization of the contingency approach to leadership involves the maturity of the follower. Hersey and Blanchard (1988) contend that leader behavior should be based on the extent to which organization members have the skills and maturity to accomplish specific organizational tasks. The Hersey and Blanchard model is based on the interplay among three elements: 1) the extent to which the leader gives direction (task behavior), 2) the extent to which the leader provides socio-emotional support (relationship behavior), and 3) the extent to which the followers exhibit "maturity." Maturity is defined in relation to a specific task and is the capability to set high and attainable goals, to take responsibility, and the level of education and/or experience of the individual or group. An individual or group may be very mature on one task but very low on another. The basic concept suggests that for the low maturity situation the leader begins with both high task and high relationship behavior. As the level of maturity increases, the leader should decrease task behavior and increase or maintain relationship behavior. As maturity reaches the "above average" level, the leader may reduce relationship behavior as well because the more mature individual or group will perceive the reduction as an indication of the leader's confidence. It should be evident that this approach to leadership places great emphasis on the development of the individual and group in an effort to accomplish organizational goals.

Elementary principals should adjust their leadership style from school task to school task depending on how skilled and mature the faculty is in accomplishing the task. If teachers are very good at maintaining pupil discipline in their classrooms, the principal should either practice a participative (low task, high relationship) or a delegative (low task, low relationship) style. However, if the faculty is at a loss on how to evaluate or revise the elementary science curriculum, the principal should exhibit either a telling (high task, low relationship) or a selling (high task, high relationship) leadership style. This contingency approach to leadership can be applied on an individual staff member basis as well as to a group.

The Hersey and Blanchard contingency model differs from Fiedler's model in important ways. While the latter has two basic task and relations oriented leadership styles, the former also includes the delegating and selling styles. The elementary principal then should be flexible enough to apply as many as four leadership styles. In addition, Hersey and Blanchard contend that leadership styles can be learned whereas Fiedler's model postulates that leadership style is grounded in the personality. Hence, the personal flexibility necessary to practice various leadership styles may not be amenable to training. Students of elementary school administration should determine the appropriate leadership style(s) as they apply theory to practice while working with the cases and vignettes in this book.

These brief discussions of several conceptualizations of the contingency approach to leadership are designed to merely introduce situational leadership models to students of elementary school administration. Readers are urged to go to the actual sources listed in the references at this chapter's end for more definitive and thorough presentations of the several conceptualizations.

THE HUMAN RESOURCES PERSPECTIVE

An elementary school principal who believes that his or her major function in the school is to encourage both staff and students to become the best persons they are capable of being has a human resources perspective on life. When that principal organizes the human and material resources of the school so that an open climate is fostered, staff and students will find they can overcome all but a few obstacles to their professional and personal development respectively. The human resources principal holds that individual student and teacher goals, objectives, and motives must be promoted and given full opportunity to be fulfilled. Further, such a principal understands that either articulated or ambiguous organization goals are surely advanced when people needs in the school are met.

Human Relations vs. Human Resources

The distinction between human relations and human resources theory has been set forth by Miles (1965). The major objective of the human relations approach is to make the members of the organization "feel a useful and important part of the overall effort." The human relations approach seeks to develop a cooperative and cohesive work force. The principal gives up some control in order to "buy" the support of teachers by allowing them to participate in the decision-making process.

The human resources model views all members of the organization as "reservoirs of untapped resources." The goal of participation is not to "buy" the cooperation of teachers but to improve decision making. This position holds that the best decisions are often made by those persons most directly involved. Further, those persons may also make decisions more efficiently.

Miles discovered that while administrators espoused the virtues of the human resources model and sought its utilization by their superiors, they actually applied the human relations model with their own subordinates. According to Miles, these administrators apparently lacked the basic trust and confidence in their subordinates necessary to the human resources model. One explanation offered is that administrators often regard control as a scarce resource and fear losing it. Human resources theory rejects this view and asserts that control is actually increased when administrators enable subordinates to develop self-control while they are, at the same time, encouraged to be creative.

An important development in the thought which led to the human resources approach was McGregor's concept (1960) of "Theory X" and "Theory Y". The traditional view of people and work was described by McGregor and called "Theory X". This view held that people were basically uninterested in work, needed to be controlled if not coerced, were irresponsible, and incapable of much creativity. By contrast, McGregor suggested a view which he believed to be supported by modern social science research and he called this revised view "Theory Y". It stood in sharp contrast to "Theory X" and held that people desire to find intrinsic interest and worth in their work, are self-directing, strive to be responsible, and, given support and resources, are capable of considerable creativity. While later critics argued that his view was too dichotomous and that in reality people are a mixture of both "Theory X" and "Theory Y", McGregor's work was influential in the movement towards a more positive understanding of human work and management.

Rensis Likert (1967) developed a model for describing organizational variables, evaluating those variables and grouping them into four basic systems. System 1 is the "exploitive-authoritarian", System 2 the "benevolent-authoritarian", System 3 the "consultive" and System 4 the "participative". Systems 1 and 2 can be described together as they both are characterized by high levels of control by centralized hierarchies which result in low loyalty, less cooperation, low performance, and more conflict. System 3 organizations are characterized as more adequate in production and performance with more favorable attitudes and relationships. However, they have not reached the level of System 4 which has the greatest potential to maximize both the individual and the organization. System 4 organizations are decentralized, have flexible and open communication, are people-centered, and have high levels of participation in decision making. The System 4 organization is clearly an example of a human resources approach to management. The Likert model is useful for elementary school principals who wish to evaluate their own practices and their school's or district's standing in human resources terms.

Later Conceptualizations of the Human Resources Approach

The productivity of Japanese business has been recently examined in human resources terms (Ouchi 1981). One form of group participation in Japanese organizations that reflects the human resources approach is the Quality Circle (QC). A QC consists of a small group of employees doing similar or related work. The QC process has four major phases. In the first phase, the QC members brainstorm, collect data, and suggest cause and effect. They then prepare solutions and recommendations. The supervisor considers the recommendations and reaches a decision. The last but very important step is to provide recognition and rewards for the QC members. In principle, participation is voluntary, however, peer pressure may be needed and can result in high rates of participation.

This concept can be applied to the whole faculty of a small elementary school or the teachers in the intermediate grades. The teachers would meet regularly (about an hour three or four times per month) to identify, analyze, and produce solutions to school problems. The principal usually serves as the chairperson, but a teacher could also be chairperson of the group. Since financial incentives are an important part of the QC process, elementary school principals, in cooperation with the Central Office, would need to develop or determine rewards for successful task accomplishment. Some type of bonus or merit award that has a financial basis to it seems necessary if the QC process is to be as effective as it appears to be in Japan.

Another analysis of organizational leadership reflective of the human resources approach involves the concept of "corporate cultures". Deal and Kennedy (1984), in their study of highly successful businesses, discovered that leaders had created a guiding vision which shaped the shared values in the organization. The values were known and shared by everyone in the organization, from top to bottom. The leader paid a great deal of attention to the development and maintenance of the resulting "culture". These successful leaders recognize the need of people to feel a sense of pride, belonging, and ownership in the enterprise; that people are more creative when given more freedom; and that all of this leads to increased productivity and better quality. Companies which make people feel special and cared for are rewarded by a bond between the company and the employees which also results in remarkable increases in productivity and quality. Being a part of such an organization gives meaning to people's lives. Work becomes more than a job.

Elementary school principals would do well to examine their own school "culture" to understand how it either enhances or deters the qualities described above. Does the school's culture indicate the values of caring and belonging? Are those values evident throughout the school in teachers, students, and noninstructional personnel? Does everyone feel a sense of pride in the school and their work? The elementary school principal should also understand the culture of the school in order to know how to change it. Successful leaders are makers and shapers of organizational culture.

Peters and Waterman (1982) discovered what they considered to be eight attributes of "excellent" and innovative companies. Those attributes were:

1. A bias for action - though analytical in their decision making, these companies are not paralyzed by it;
2. Close to the customer - learn from the people who are served;
3. Autonomy and entrepreneurship - encourage practical risk taking and support good efforts;
4. Productivity through people - all employees are treated as the well source of quality and productivity;
5. Hands-on, value driven - focus is on results and all employees are close to the product;
6. Stick to the knitting - never acquire a venture that you do not know how to operate;
7. Simple form, lean staff - companies are structurally simple and numbers of top level administrators are minimal;
8. Simultaneous loose-tight properties - autonomy exists down to level of implementation yet a strong set of core values guides everyone.

While these attributes will not be discussed in detail here, they may be suggestive to the reader. Attribute 4, "productivity through people," for example, is especially noteworthy from the human resources perspective. As one corporate founder said, when speaking about what was most important, it was "our respect for the individual." Another said every worker is "seen as a source of ideas, not just a pair of hands." The excellent companies allow wide latitude to employees at all levels in the organization while, at the same time, they are fanatic about the core values of the organization.

While there is not a simple one-to-one transfer of these findings to elementary schools, there is much in the work of Peters and Waterman that is instructive for principals and school executives. For example, attribute 1, "a bias for action," would warn against endless and indecisive faculty or committee meetings, a frequent complaint in schools. "Close to the customer," attribute 2, would suggest keeping the focus on students and their needs. Upon reflection, each attribute offers something which can be applied to schools.

The work of Deal-Kennedy and Peters-Waterman has a common starting point. It is that we must move beyond "rational" management, the so-called scientific management which began with Frederick Taylor in the early 1900's. Deal and Kennedy are advocates of what they identify as "symbolic" management. Managers focus on the values, culture and drama of the organization. Peters and Waterman speak of "managing ambiguity and paradox" and suggest Darwinian evolutionary theory may be useful in understanding how organizations interact with the environment. There are exciting possibilities when these perspectives are applied to elementary schools. Upon reflection, much of what an elementary school principal can do is symbolic, culture-shaping, values-affirming. School cultures are certainly in a state of evolution as they attempt to adjust or adapt, as living organisms, to the social and political environment and trends at the local, state, and national levels.

IMPLEMENTING THE HUMAN RESOURCES APPROACH THROUGH STAFF DEVELOPMENT

Staff development is a necessary requirement of and an inherent part of the human resources approach. Since the quality of teaching relies on growth in knowledge, research, creativity, and practice, staff development is a necessity for schools. Traditionally, staff development, or the upgrading of professional personnel, is treated as an expense to a school system. However, a more productive teaching staff is an asset and, therefore, justifies the expense. The elementary school principal should take the initiative in building a staff development program that encourages teachers to become the best persons and professionals they are capable of being.

The concept of staff development is normally perceived as an individual matter. Ideally what is done in staff development, also known as in-service training, should bring about direct benefit to teachers in human resources terms. An individualized development program for each teacher is an excellent ideal. However, needed economy of effort and funds may require that staff development be undertaken in groups. Though a teacher may have a group experience, the teacher can grow from the experience. Either way, elementary school principals should allow teachers to have maximum input in determining the content of the school's staff development program.

Human resources supervision can be easily observed. The elementary school principal allows the staff maximum freedom and opportunity to plan, organize, and implement staff development programs, curricular changes, instructional improvements, and pupil personnel policies. The elementary school principal enriches the job situation for teachers by providing advancement/growth opportunities, responsibility, recognition, and autonomy to teachers. The participatory conflict management and decision-making practices discussed in Chapters I and II are prevalent in the school on both a short- and long-term basis. Professional advancement/growth is encouraged because the principal has a rational belief in the potential of the staff as a group and is fully committed to each staff member's self-development. Human resources supervision does not necessarily subordinate organizational goals to individual goals; rather, it actually promotes organizational goals by directly influencing the fulfillment of individual teacher needs and interests through job enrichment.

SITE-BASED DECISION MAKING AND HUMAN RESOURCES

Site-based management lends itself to the human resources approach to the supervision of school personnel. Site-based management calls on all those who have a stake in the local education enterprise to participate in serious decision making (hiring, terminating, budgeting, building/renovating, programming, restructuring, etc.). Ostensibly, decisions are made by persons closest to the concerns, issues, and problems of a school rather than central office personnel or district-wide policy makers. In reality, however, most site-based management efforts retain central control of financing, budgeting, information, and certain other support functions such as purchasing, food service, and transportation. That may leave programming or curriculum development, some personnel matters such as principal selection and retention, and minimal resource allocation (e.g., per pupil budgeted monies per school) in the hands of a representative site-based committee or council.

James E. Mitchell (1990), superintendent of the Northglenn, Colorado school district, identified a number of "blocks" to successful school site-based management. First, there are school district policies emphasizing central control. Next the principal is perceived by teachers and others as a manipulator of the site-based management process in order to retain authority. Further, head teachers or grade level chairpersons may limit involvement because they do not wish to share decision-making power with their colleagues. Also, the master collective bargaining agreement may be perceived as an instrument for past practice and the status quo. Still another blocker could be the school board itself. Boards can be suspicious of any attempt to "dilute" their own or their administrators' authority and power. Finally, the superintendent and the central office can impede progress on shared decision making because of their traditional control of the school district's finances, information, and other matters.

These "blocks" each tend to support the human relations approach to supervising people and managing material resources. They reflect the suspicious view of human nature so succinctly identified in McGregor's Theory X. Once the elementary principal identifies these "blocks" he or she can act to minimize their effects in the school.

As a human resources advocate, the elementary principal will ask teachers, staff, parents, school community, and students, where applicable, to take some risks. He or she will urge them to venture along new and uncharted paths, to expose themselves to *both* the successes and problems of the school, diagnose shortcomings, prescribe remedies, and then participate in implementing the remedies. Finally, the principal will ask, indeed, encourage the group's assessment of what has occurred and then repeat the decision-making process on matters of importance to the school. As people participate more fully in the life of the school, they will gain confidence in themselves as participants and decision makers and they will grow in knowledge and practice. In short, they will have achieved "ownership" of the educational enterprise and the commitments that go along with it.

For the personal confidence building and professional growth to flower, the elementary principal must work along at least two fronts. One front involves his or her efforts to minimize the "blocks" or act as the buffer between the local school community and the blocking agents and perceptions that restrain site-based decision making. Glickman (1990) discussed "the seven ironies of school empowerment." Generally, as the school improves as a result of widely participative decision making, internal and external critics will increasingly minimize/question its accomplishments. The elementary principal needs to understand the ironies in order to manage them.

The second front involves the elementary principal's efforts to assist teachers, and, in keeping with site-based management principles, other members of the local school community to become the best persons they are capable of being. In that respect, the school site becomes the focal point of human growth and development in the community.

Site-based management has been defined as a form of decentralization identifying the individual school as the focus of improvement and reallocating decision making to it as the chief vehicle by which improvements can occur (Malen, Ogawa, and Kranz, 1990). Therefore, much discretion and formal authority are given to the local school.

Malen, Ogawa, and Kranz have concluded that site-based management has yet to live up to its expectations. For reasons already stated by Conely and Bacharach (1990) and others (Glickman, 1990;

David, 1989), site-based management will be difficult to implement. The difficulty includes the entrenched traditional norms of the school where principals administer policy, teachers instruct, and parents provide support. We contend, however, that the human resources principal has the better chance of succeeding in a site-based management situation because of his or her rational faith in the ability of people to take on reasonable risks/challenges, set goals and objectives, strive hard to achieve them, and pursue self-actualization to the fullest. Acting on that faith, the elementary principal can meet the obstacles to site-based management, (including his or her own reservations concerning loss of influence) persevere, and, over time, observe the school's improvement.

SOME TEACHERS WON'T RESPOND—A PRINCIPAL'S CHALLENGE

An inherent assumption of human resources supervision is that all teachers are willing to work hard at teaching if they have interesting, challenging work and if the school district allows them to participate in educational decision making. However, human resources advocates also recognize that some teachers merely go "through the motions" and do not expect to get their satisfaction or "self-actualization" at work. These teachers have a variety of reasons for giving minimum effort to the job. Some are frustrated and wish they were doing something else, some feel their situation in the community or school is smothering and only desire to be severed from their present environment. Others are lethargic or "burned out" and are unable to get involved in anything professional. For some teachers, participation in educational decision making engenders too much anxiety. These immature teachers in Hersey and Blanchard's terms would probably be too reluctant to assume the necessary responsibility and would retreat to those activities which provide for personal security. These teachers will need more direction from the elementary school principal.

The human resources approach offers a challenge to the elementary school principal. Consistently maintaining an environment where interesting, challenging, and purposeful tasks are available to the teacher is not easy. A task must be directed toward the achievement of a goal. The principal needs to be unusually creative, demanding, helpful, observant, and well-organized to set goals or manage conflicts that enhance the efficiency and effectiveness of the elementary school.

USE OF THE TEXT IN TERMS OF THE HUMAN RESOURCES PERSPECTIVE

Students of elementary school administration should view the case studies and vignettes from a human resources perspective. Students should find that conflict resolution is more easily obtained when the fulfillment of people needs/interests is focused on first and organizational concerns second. Too often in school administration, the reverse is practiced to the detriment of both the organization and the people in it. The contingency approach to elementary school administration should help the leader to match people with other appropriate situational factors so that the people may be most productive for themselves and the school. In this way, the human resources perspective and the contingency approach reinforce each other and provide the elementary principal with a powerful means to leadership success.

As the following vignettes and cases are studied and discussed, students should attempt to identify and become cognizant of the situational factors in each problem or conflict and utilize the contingency approach. Morse and Lorsch's triad of interrelated situational factors (task, structure, and people) should help students discover those same factors in each case study and vignette. Students should understand that their ability to work with and modify, if necessary, either their hypothetical leadership style or the situational factors inherent in the cases and vignettes or both may determine how they will be perceived by themselves and others as potentially successful elementary school leaders.

ORGANIZATION OF THE VIGNETTES AND CASES

The vignettes which follow in Chapters IV–VII are arranged according to particular task and relationship responsibilities of the principal. Chapter IV, "Professional Staff Relations," deals with one of the most important aspects of the principal's work. Professional staff are most central to the educational purpose of the school and the ones with whom the principal needs to develop a cooperative, working relationship. Chapter V, "Noninstructional Staff Relations," emphasizes the importance of the support staff to the operation of the school. Chapter VI, "Relationships with Pupils," moves to a central concern of the building administrator, the relationships among students and between students and teachers and completes the in-house constituencies of the principal. Chapter VII, "School-Community Relations," "broadens the focus to the external environment of the school and the variety of challenges it often poses. Chapter VIII, "District-Wide Relationships: The Cases," the final chapter of the book, provides detail case material which requires the principal to consider problems within the context of the school district as well as the individual school.

ADAPTING THE VIGNETTES AND CASES TO OTHER LEVELS

Many of the vignettes and cases in this book may be adapted to middle/junior high school and/or high school levels. Some vignettes already deal with problems at the sixth to eighth grades level. Some of the issues or problems are common to any school level.

To adapt a vignette or case, instructors and students should change the name of the school, the grade levels, the positions (teachers, principals, students, etc.), and possibly other factors that would give the problem or issue another level focus. Generally, the discussion questions following each vignette or case would remain the same. The concepts introduced in the initial chapters could apply to any school level.

A high school adaptation of "Teachers' Personal Freedom Jeopardized" on page 106 could involve the following change: Mrs. Yule would now be principal of McCalley Senior High School. The rest of the vignette could stay the same.

Another secondary adaptation could occur with "A 'Letter to the Editor' " on page 85. A junior high school newspaper could be substituted for the reference to the elementary school newspaper. The school would be Gordon Junior High. The reference to eighth grade black students could be changed to ninth grade if desired. The remainder of the vignette could stay the same.

Listed here are the vignettes and cases the authors believe could be easily adapted to the secondary level.

Vignettes

Cases

Case Study Number 7: Too Many Forces!, page 156

This listing suggests that more than 60 percent of the vignettes and more than half of the cases may be adapted to other school levels. However, the others not listed may be adapted, too, but perhaps not as easily.

REFERENCES

Kenneth Blanchard, et al., **Leadership and the One Minute Manager: Increasing Effectiveness Through Situational Leadership** (New York: William Morrow and Company, 1985).

Peter Burke, ed., **Programming for Staff Development: Fanning the Flame** (New York: Falmer Press, 1990).

Sharon C. Conely and Samuel B. Bacharack, "From School-Site Management to Participatory School-Site Management," **Phi Delta Kappan** '71, No. 7 (March 1990): 539–544.

James L. David, "Synthesis of Research on School-Based Management," **Educational Leadership** 46 (May, 1989): 45–53.

Stanley M. Davis, **Managing Corporate Culture** (Cambridge, Mass.: Ballinger Publishing Company, 1985).

Terrence E. Deal and Allan A. Kennedy, **Corporate Cultures: The Rites and Rituals of Corporate Life** (Reading, Mass: Addison-Wesley Publishing Co., 1984).

Fred E. Fiedler, "Style or Circumstance: The Leadership Enigmas," **Psychology Today** 2, No. 10 (March, 1969): 38–43.

Michael Fullan, **The New Meaning of Educational Change,** 2nd ed. (New York: Columbia Teachers College, 1991).

Phillip E. Gates, Kenneth H. Blanchard, and Paul Hersey, "Diagnosing Educational Leadership Problems: A Situational Approach," **Educational Leadership** 33, No. 5 (1976): 348–54.

Carl D. Glickman, "Pushing School Reform to a New Edge: The Seven Ironies of School Empowerment," **Phi Delta Kappan** 72, No. 1 (September, 1990): 68–75.

Ben M. Harris, **Improving Staff Performance Through In-Service Education** (Boston: Allyn and Bacon, Inc., 1980).

Philip K. Harris, **High Performance Leadership** (New York: Scott, Foresman, 1989).

Paul Hersey and Kenneth Blanchard, **Management of Organizational Behavior,** 5th ed. (Englewood Cliffs, N.J.: Prentice-Hall, 1988).

Wayne K. Hoy and Cecil G. Miskel, **Educational Administration: Theory, Research, and Practice,** 3rd ed. (New York: McGraw-Hill, 1986).

Wayne K. Hoy, C. J. Tarter, and Robert B. Kottkamp, **Open Schools/Healing Schools: Measuring Organizational Climate** (Newbury Park, CA: The Corwin Press, Inc. 1991).

Robert B. Kottkamp, "The Principal As Cultural Leader," **Planning and Changing** (Fall, 1981): 152–160.

Dennis J. Kravetz, **The Human Resources Revolution: Implementing Progressive Management Practices for Bottom-Line Success** (San Francisco: Jossey-Bass, 1988).

Robert Levering, **A Great Place to Work: What Makes Some Employers So Good** (New York: Random House, 1988).

Harry Levinson, ed., **Designing and Managing Your Career: Advice from the Harvard Business Review** (Boston: Harvard Business School Press, 1988).

Ann Lieberman and Lynne Miller, eds., **Staff Development for Education in the '90s,** 2nd ed. (New York: Columbia Teachers College Press, 1991).

Rensis Likert, **The Human Organization: Its Management and Value** (New York: McGraw-Hill Book Co., 1967).

George H. Litwin and Robert A. Stringer, Jr., **Motivation and Organizational Climate** (Boston: Harvard University, Division of Research, Graduate School of Business, 1968).

Charles K. Long, "Quality Circles in the Schools: Problems and Solutions," **Education** 107, No. 1 (Fall, 1986): 55–57.

Betty Malen, Rodney T. Ogawa, and Jennifer Kraz, "Unfulfilled Promises: Evidence Says Site-Based Management Hindered by Many Factors," **The School Administrator** 47, No. 2 (February, 1990): 30, 32, 53–56, and 59.

Douglas McGregor, **The Human Side of Enterprise** (New York: McGraw-Hill Book Co., 1960).

Raymond E. Miles, "Human Relations or Human Resources?", **Harvard Business Review** 43, No. 4 (July–August, 1965): 148–163.

James E. Mitchell, "Coaxing Staff from Cages for Site-Based Decisions to Fly," **The School Administrator** 47, No. 2 (February, 1990): 23–24, and 26.

John J. Morse and Jay W. Lorsch, "Beyond Theory Y," **Harvard Business Review** 48, No. 3 (May/June, 1970): 61–68.

Burt Nanus, **The Leader's Edge: The Seven Keys to Leadership in a Turbulent World** (Chicago: Contemporary Books, 1989).

Daniel C. Neale, William J. Bailey, and Billy E. Ross, **Strategies for School Improvement** (Boston, Mass.: Allyn and Bacon, Inc., 1981).

William G. Ouchi, **Theory Z: How American Business Can Meet the Japanese Challenge** (Reading, Mass: Addison-Wesley Publishing Co., 1981).

Tom Peters, **Thriving on Chaos: Handbook for a Management Revolution** (New York: Alfred A. Knopf, 1987).

Tom J. Peters and Nancy K. Austin, **A Passion for Excellence** (New York: Warner Books, 1986).

Thomas J. Peters and Robert H. Waterman, Jr., **In Search of Excellence: Lessons from America's Best Run Companies** (New York: Warner Books, 1982).

Thomas J. Sergiovanni, **Value-Added Leadership: How to Get Extraordinary Performance in Schools** (San Diego: Harcourt, Brace, Jovanovich, Inc., 1989).

Thomas J. Sergiovanni and Fred D. Carver, **The New School Executive: A Theory of Administration** (New York: Harper and Row, 1980).

Thomas J. Sergiovanni and Robert J. Starratt, **Supervision: Human Perspectives,** 3rd ed. (New York: McGraw-Hill Book Co., 1983).

Albert Shapero, **Managing Professional People: Understanding Creative Performance** (New York: Macmillan/Free Press, 1985).

Gregory Shea, "Quality Circles: The Danger of Bottled Change," **Sloan Management Review** 27, No. 3 (Spring, 1986): 33–46.

VIGNETTES AND CASES

Professional Staff
Relations

To survive, the elementary school principal must promote good internal relations among staff members and between teachers and students and their parents. Human relations skills assist the principal to move teachers to accomplish school goals and objectives. Human resources skills enable the principal to motivate teachers to strive and reach their own professional goals within the context of the school's goals. Human resources skills are superior to human relations in that **both** the school's and the professional staff's interests are promoted by the principal. The elementary principal is continually interacting with the faculty on a face-to-face basis and is, therefore, most responsible for developing a healthy and productive school culture.

Poor professional staff relations undermine support for the school and create hard feelings among the significant others in the school's community. Usually poor staff relations are associated with inadequate supervision, ineffective instructional practices and classroom management procedures, conflicting ethical conduct, and unclear division of responsibilities. Vague statements of philosophy and objectives tend to encourage dissension among teachers and between teachers and their students' parents.

Inadequate instructional leadership is reflected in the school when the principal acts in administrative ways through impersonal memos, written or verbal directives, unilateral decision making, lack of physical presence, and "closed door" polices. Adequate, indeed, successful instructional leadership requires the elementary principal to act in supervisory ways through other persons, namely the school's professional staff. Thus, the principal will involve the staff prior to setting standards for acceptable teaching, engage in mutual or joint idea sharing, pool human and material resources in consultation with the staff, collegially define and establish school goals, and coordinate services in the school. Disunity, rivalry, and petty differences are more likely to be dissipated or moderated when the elementary principal works with and through the professional staff to accomplish the school's instructional goals.

When the elementary principal acts in a supervisory way, division of responsibility problems can be minimized. Typical elementary school staff-related problems such as heavy class loads or preparations and too many time consuming extra duties are more easily and equitably mediated or remediated as the principal involves the staff in problem solving.

The school's informal organization can and usually does affect professional staff relations. Teachers of a particular subject, grade level, minority or ethnic group, or general age group may band together for their own protection and interests. These informal groups may direct their nonclassroom activities to improve their group position to the neglect of the school's goals and interests. The elementary principal who is willing and able to penetrate the informal organizational structure and its communications network through supervisory behavior, that is, working with and through people, will have fewer difficulties with informal special interest groups in the school.

Below are some guiding questions that should help the reader better understand the situations described in the professional staff relations vignettes.

> Is the reason for the conflict inadequate school policy? No policy?
>
> Is there an unacceptable degree of inequity in the conflict situation?
>
> Are only insufficient choices possible to resolve the conflict?
>
> Does the conflict involve professional discretion versus organizational or community expectations?

School Organization And Policy

THE WRONG FOUR

In the first week of October, enrollment at Hancock Elementary School had reached 800. Transfer students were assigned to their proper level and then placed in the class with the lowest enrollment.

Since the school organization was based upon heterogeneous grouping, the random assignment of pupils did not affect the school's objectives. Each grade had three teachers.

During the third week of October, Mrs. Smith told the principal,
Mr. Catou, that Mr. Green and she each had six more students than
Mrs. Brown, the other fifth grade teacher. Mr. Catou checked his
records and discovered that Mrs. Smith was correct. Mrs. Smith suggested that if no new students were assigned by November, that she
and Mr. Green each send two students to Mrs. Brown to even class
sizes. Mr. Catou agreed. No new students entered the fifth grade,
and, on November 1, the principal sent a request to Mrs. Smith and
Mr. Green to each send one girl and one boy to Mrs. Brown's class.
A copy of the note was sent to Mrs. Brown.

A week after the students had been assigned to Mrs. Brown, Mr.
Catou found a note from the secretary stating that Mrs. Brown would
be in to see him in the afternoon.

That afternoon a very hostile Mrs. Brown entered his office. She
stated that the four children she received from the two teachers were
not only reading at a third grade level but were also incorrigible.
Their behavior was the worst in the room, and she felt it unfair that
her class was a dumping ground for the other teachers' discipline
problems. She wanted the four students returned to the other teachers, and she would expect four normal students selected by the
guidance teacher or the principal.

QUESTIONS FOR DISCUSSION

1. What decision-making method did the principal use in this instance? Was it appropriate in your view? Why or why not?
2. How might Mr. Catou have proceeded differently?
3. Describe the culture of this school in terms of Deal and
   Kennedy's conclusions about highly successful organizations.
4. What grounds might Mrs. Brown have for her objections?
5. What might Mr. Catou do to prevent a similar problem from
   developing in the future? What factors would he need to consider in the process?

HONESTY IS THE BEST POLICY?

The print-out for the results of the third grade achievement tests
indicated the children were making excellent progress. As the principal sorted the children into the three third grade classes, he was
somewhat surprised at the results. It appeared that the room with
the highest mean score was Ms. Bell's, a teacher with only three

years experience. The classes were heterogeneously organized. The principal attributed good teaching as a significant factor. Perhaps the district's strong accountability and monitoring scheme was working after all. The principal emphasized the district's policy and maybe these were the results. His visits to Ms. Bell's classroom, however, did not seem to square with the results. She seemed too free, disorganized, lax on discipline, had too many games, and wasn't even close to getting through the course of study.

The principal wondered what Mrs. Kapro would say. Her class had always scored the highest. She had always said that students learn through good teaching to do what they do. The more time they spend on actually doing school work, the more they learn. That's a truth and who could argue with her twenty-two years of experience.

The next day Mrs. Kapro came to see the principal. The gist of the conversation was that Ms. Bell had been frightened of the district's accountability procedures and had been faking her students' results during the school year. She had acquired a copy of the achievement test and taught the test including the answers to the children two weeks before its administration.

QUESTIONS FOR DISCUSSION

1. Would you investigate Mrs. Kapro's charges? Why or why not? What conflict-handling style should the principal apply in this instance?
2. If the charge proved to be true, how would you proceed from that point?
3. If the charge proved to be false, how would you proceed?
4. Is competition between teachers appropriate? Explain.
5. Would the principal's observations of Ms. Bell's classroom support Mrs. Kapro's charges? Why or why not? What decision making trap(s) should the principal watch out for in this situation?
6. What assumptions about learning are held by Mrs. Kapro and, to some degree, by the principal? Do you agree or disagree with those assumptions? How would agreement or disagreement affect your response?

MAKING A TRADE

Mr. Pesar, principal of Oak Elementary School, had calculated the projected enrollment for September. It appeared that the student population was stable. However, more students were in the sixth grade while the number of students in the second grade had decreased.

Mrs. Johnson, twenty-three years of experience, Mrs. Lane, fifteen years of experience, and Mrs. Meyers, one year of experience, were second grade teachers. In the past three years since he became principal of the school, Mr. Pesar had been constantly getting requests from parents to change their children from Mrs. Lane's class, and, wherever possible, he satisfied the parents' requests.

The supervisory visits and conferences he had with Mrs. Lane did not seem to change her behavior. She had been assigned the upper third of the second graders and treated them as if they were in the army and she was their first sergeant. Her constant reply to Mr. Pesar's suggestions that she be more sensitive and less authoritarian was that the children needed strong discipline and structure—particularly now since the parents did not provide it at home.

Mr. Pesar thought that Mrs. Meyers, the first year teacher, was outstanding. She has all the attributes that one would want in a primary grades teacher. Perhaps the sixth graders could better tolerate Mrs. Lane's rigid teaching.

The following week Mrs. Meyers asked Mr. Pesar, the principal, "Since I have the least tenure, I guess I will be going to the sixth grade. I really prefer where I am at, but I will take it and do the best I can." Mr. Pesar replied, "I don't know what next September's teachers' assignments are. I want to think about them."

Later in the week Mr. Raney, the eighth grade science teacher and a faculty leader, stopped Mr. Pesar in the hall. "I hear you are not sure who is going to be shifted to the sixth grade. Most of us know that there are some problems with Mrs. Lane. If you destroy our tradition of seniority having first choice, you will be making a number of enemies and probably have a bad effect on morale." Mr. Pesar then entered his office and found a memo from the superintendent asking that teacher assignments for next year be sent to the central office in three days.

QUESTIONS FOR DISCUSSION

1. What category of conflict does the principal face here? What are the major elements of the conflict?
2. As the principal, what decision-making steps would you take? What factors would influence your thinking? Would you make the assignments yourself? Consult with others? If so, with whom?
3. Would you accept Mrs. Meyers' offer? Why or why not?
4. Apart from the assignment issue, how would you manage Mrs. Lane's resistance to supervision? Would you apply a human relations or human resources approach here? Explain your choice.

5. How would you relate to Mr. Raney and the informal structure of the school? Is Mr. Raney a potential "linking pin"? Why or why not? Will the informal structure be helpful in your efforts or obstructive? Why do you think so?

6. Consider a win/win strategy that has as its goal the maximizing of growth for both teachers and students.

THAT HELPLESS FEELING

Mr. Williams, principal of Sims Elementary School, was pondering about Mrs. Karr. Since her husband died four years ago, her teaching performance declined greatly. She had been an outstanding teacher—creative, sensitive, organized, understanding, flexible, and, above all, healthy and punctual. Now he considered her barely acceptable when she was in the classroom. She already had been absent for forty-seven days and tardy fifteen times and it was only March.

Mr. Williams wondered if the sixty-three year old Mrs. Karr was going to resign at the end of the year. She still had eighty-three days of sick leave left. Before her husband died, she never missed a day or came a minute late.

A few parents had called to ask him to change their children to a different room. They were not upset by her teaching, but by her attendance. They said their children were not getting an education when substitutes were in the room so frequently. When Mr. Williams had previously talked with Mrs. Karr in October about her absenteeism, she had replied, "Look at my record. Do you think I would take any sick days if I didn't need them?" She then missed the next three days of school.

Mr. Williams felt stumped. He could not reject the doctor's medical excuse that had explained Mrs. Karr's sickness for the last five days, but could he tolerate the continued absences not only for the remainder of this school year but possibly for the next few years?

QUESTIONS FOR DISCUSSION

1. How would a human relations and a human resources approach differ in this instance? Explain.

2. How does one weigh past service against present nonperformance? What are the ethical, professional, legal, and community issues involved in such cases?

3. What category of conflict applies to Mrs. Karr's situation? What supervisory steps might enhance the opportunity for Mrs. Karr to realize her professional goals and, at the same time, meet the educational interests of the school?

4. What resources are available and what policies apply in your district to assist teachers with medical and personal problems which deter performance? What resources ought to be available and what policies ought to apply?

5. Do teachers experience career stages as they do life stages? Is Mrs. Karr at the end of her career? Why or why not?

NEGOTIATING A PROBLEM OF SEXIST VALUES

Mr. Kane was wondering whether he had been a teacher too long. Working in a team teaching situation made him have too much contact with other teachers and students. He enjoyed the interaction with other teachers, but he felt too much time was spent on planning.

A staffing for Dick Bronson was planned for today. Dick was ten years old, large for his age, very bright, extroverted, and a born leader. However, he was always getting into trouble. In many cases, his poor behavior was contagious and the other students aped him. When given an assignment, he would be the first in the class to finish it albeit sometimes sloppily. Mr. Kane thought Dick to be a normal child with developmental problems normal to his age. He said, "I don't see why we need a staffing on Dick. He is just all boy." At this comment, Alice Clark replied angrily, "That's the trouble—when Dick says he doesn't like to play with the girls, regards them as sissies, gets into a lot of trouble, or knocks the primary children around, you say he is all boy. Your male chauvinistic attitude excuses and reinforces his bad behavior. You may be able to tolerate it but I can't. As long as we are in a team teaching situation, we need to decide what we expect of our students."

Mr. Kane replied, "That certainly is one of our problems. Your feminism is giving you tunnel vision. All you look at is how we should deal with student roles. As a result, we spend endless time on this subject rather than dealing with the students' achievement problems." John Kane and Alice Clark looked at the principal, Mr. James, and waited for him to speak.

QUESTIONS FOR DISCUSSION

1. If you were the principal, what would you say? Would you be inclined to take a human relations rather than a human resources approach here? Explain.
2. What questions surface about each teacher as you consider their statements? What supervisory issues are suggested by these questions?
3. Would you define this situation as an attitudinal conflict or a relationship conflict? Why?
4. Are Mr. Kane and Ms. Clark engaged in a win/lose negotiations strategy here? Explain. Can these two teachers find a shared value? What might it be?
5. As principal, how would you follow up after the meeting, if at all? If you followed up, what decision-making model would you apply to this situation? Explain.

CHANGING POLICY OR CHANGING TEACHERS?

Mr. Ladd, principal of Hillside School in a middle class suburb, had actively supported an innovative program of individualized instruction and team teaching. Careful evaluation included in the program design indicated the students did slightly better in achievement. The teachers in the program were very favorable towards it; discipline problems had decreased significantly, and the general climate of the school had improved. Now after three years of operation, sixteen of the twenty teachers were enthusiastically committed to the program.

The remaining four teachers, all tenured, rejected individualization on the grounds that children needed strong structure, were too young to make decisions about their learning, and needed standards. Team teaching was too difficult for these teachers because of personality clashes. Mr. Ladd started the program on a voluntary basis with one team and had expected that the success of the program would be enough evidence that all the teachers would want to join it. He began to wonder if he was too indecisive in determining the boundaries of teacher autonomy. As April approached, he was becoming increasingly unhappy with the islands of rigidity in the school. On one afternoon, he took down five educational administration texts from his shelf and a book on organizational change. Again, he began to plan for teacher acceptance of change.

QUESTIONS FOR DISCUSSION

1. What category of conflict is occurring here? Does this conflict involve professional discretion versus organizational or community expectations?
2. How much latitude is appropriate for the individual teacher? Who decides and how? Should the principal be guided by the authority-freedom continuum in this instance? Why or why not?
3. What specific steps could the principal take to enlist the support of the remaining teachers?
4. Would transfer of the remaining four teachers be an option? Would it be wise? Why or why not? Support your answer with a human resources approach. A corporate culture approach.
5. If you could suggest a theory or model of organizational change which Mr. Ladd might find in his book, what would it be? Would any of the contingency approaches or models be helpful? Why or why not?
6. Are the recalcitrant teachers subscribers to Theory X or Theory Y? Why do you think so?

A PARTY—INDEED!

Mrs. O'Day, a new seventh grade teacher, was surprised by her class on St. Patrick's Day with a class party. All the students had been planning for weeks, and everyone contributed with homemade goodies or store-bought treats. A few students had brought some Irish folk song records, and, as a part of the entertainment, one student was going to teach the other students an Irish jig. This party appeared to be a good indication that Mrs. O'Day had been able to establish excellent rapport with this difficult class.

The assistant principal, Mr. O'Reilly, walked into the room while the party was in progress. He informed the teacher that it was against the school policy to hold parties during class time. Parties were only permissible during the Christmas holiday and Halloween. Mrs. O'Day told the assistant principal she would not cancel the party. She wanted to see the principal. She told the assistant principal to supervise the party. She would be right back. Mrs. O'Day then left for the principal's office before Mr. O'Reilly could respond.

QUESTIONS FOR DISCUSSION

1. How would you respond if you were the assistant principal? Which of the three organizational dilemmas is the assistant principal confronted with here? Explain.

2. Did Mr. O'Reilly handle the situation appropriately? Why or why not? Did Mrs. O'Day? Why or why not?

3. How would you respond as the principal? Would the confrontation method or neutral party concept be applicable here? Explain.

4. Are there times when a school policy might be set aside for good reasons? If so, who should decide and how might such a decision be made? Do you think this was one of those times?

5. Could this impasse have been avoided? If so, how?

Instructional Practices

THE RELUCTANT TEACHER

Mrs. Grimbey, a primary level teacher for thirty-five years, found many of the modern teaching methods to be useless and a waste of time. She had not supported the principal in regard to any new programs. The primary committee had decided to use at least three different reading level texts in the second and third grades to better meet the reading levels of each student. Mrs. Grimbey had voted against the approach.

The next year she received ten copies of three different reading level texts for her room. She immediately approached the principal and explained she could not teach her class with these books. She would trade twenty books for seventeen more of the third grade text. The principal explained that primary children were to be taught in small groups. According to the students in her class, there were three different reading levels. That was why she received the three different books. Mrs. Grimbey insisted that she had never taught in groups and thought grouping to be a waste of time. "If I can't get the seventeen copies of the new text," she argued, "I will use my old reading texts."

The principal knew it was impossible to purchase seventeen more texts because the budget simply could not provide the money.

QUESTIONS FOR DISCUSSION

1. How would you characterize the relationship between Mrs. Grimbey and the principal? Which organizational dilemma has occurred here? Explain.
2. Does this reading books problem appear to be a matter of professional discretion or school policy? Why do you think so?
3. As the principal, what would you tell Mrs. Grimbey? Why? What conflict management method, the "linking pin," confrontation, or neutral party, would you most likely use in this instance?
4. What does the exchange between teacher and principal suggest for supervision objectives with Mrs. Grimbey? Does Morse and Lorsch's contingency theory provide guidance to the principal in working with this teacher? Why or why not?
5. Analyze this problem situation utilizing one of the decision-making models.

THE SUCCESSFUL SKINNERIAN

One year ago, Phillips Elementary School had attempted a token economy for rooms showing good behavior during the time spent outside of the classroom. The experiment was tried in an effort to improve the students' behavior during passing periods, up and down stairs, at recess and lunch. The rooms with the most tokens at the end of the week were rewarded.

Mr. Brown, a sixth grade teacher with eight years teaching experience, had many tokens. He set rigid rules for his room and demanded strict discipline. Recently, Mr. Hagger, a new teacher, began to win more tokens. Mr. Hagger had taught his class the meaning of responsibility and allowed his room to line up and dismiss themselves during recess and lunch time. They went up and down the stairs by themselves. Mr. Brown informed Mr. Hagger that it was against school policy to allow children to walk through the halls unattended. If he didn't obey the rules, Mr. Brown would notify the principal. Mr. Hagger ignored Mr. Brown. A week later Mr. Hagger was called down to the office.

The principal asked Mr. Hagger if he knew it was school policy to supervise classes in the halls. Mr. Hagger replied yes, but he felt that since the school was operating under a stimulus-response Skinnerian psychology, he was doing the right thing. The students had learned a particular behavior while he was supervising them. The principal had received no complaints about Mr. Hagger's students. Part of his job as a teacher was to teach students responsibility, and he felt that he needed to raise the difficulty of the tasks. According to Mr. Hagger, students learn responsibility if teachers give it to them when they believe students are prepared to cope with it. When he allowed students to self-discipline Mr. Hagger had performed what he considered to be good teaching within a particular philosophical and psychological framework. He concluded, "I am a new teacher and enjoy working here. I will do what I am told, but I do wish you would consider what I said."

QUESTIONS FOR DISCUSSION

1. What do you think of Mr. Hagger's rationale?
2. How would you respond to him as the principal? Could the Hersey-Blanchard leadership model be of help to the principal here? Why or why not?
3. What do you think of Mr. Brown's actions? What category of conflict is reflected between the two teachers? Explain.
4. What might be some of the reasons for such a school policy?
5. Would you anticipate ongoing conflict between the two teachers? If so, what conflict resolution approach would you take to minimize the strained relationships?
6. Consider the situation using the attributes of excellent organizations discovered by Peters and Waterman.

A PRINCIPAL'S HEADACHE

Mrs. Dismorid, a teacher for thirty years, was sixty-two years old. She considered herself a good teacher from the "old school." She was a strict disciplinarian with high expectations for good conduct and achievement. Her students, however, were having difficulty. There were an inordinate number of poor grades and negative comments on the report cards. The seventh and eighth grade students had complained to their parents and other faculty members.

The previous principal had a number of conferences with Mrs. Dismorid but nothing seemed to change. When Ms. Ruby, the new principal, observed the class her major criticism to Mrs. Dismorid was that she needed to spend more time explaining the material.

Recently a parent of one of the students came to see Ms. Ruby about her daughter. She said that her daughter had become a nervous wreck and was not learning anything. The daughter said that Mrs. Dismorid called her a tramp. The parent wanted her daughter transferred to another class.

Now Ms. Ruby began to think about what to do about Mrs. Dismorid's teaching style and professional attitude.

QUESTIONS FOR DISCUSSION

1. As Ms. Ruby, how would you respond to the parent? What conflict-handling style would you utilize in this situation?
2. How would you approach Mrs. Dismorid? Would you be inclined to have a human relations or a human resources perspective here? Explain.
3. Would you apply any decision-making steps to determine if the parent's accusation was correct? If substantiated, how serious would you consider the teacher's actions to be? What decision would you make in response?
4. How would you regard the supervision history of Mrs. Dismorid and what, if anything, would you do with it?
5. Would Mrs. Dismorid's age be a factor in your decision? Why or why not?
6. Can an older teacher "learn new tricks"? What does the human resources approach suggest?

WAS THE GOAL OF SELF-CONCEPT DISTORTED?

Mr. Hooker was one of the three Spanish bilingual teachers in Patterson Elementary School where 15 percent of the student population was Hispanic. He was totally committed to upgrading his students' chances for upward mobility. When one entered a conversation with Mr. Hooker, he constantly quoted figures such as 40 percent of Spanish-surnamed students were dropouts in high school between the tenth and twelfth grades in the district.

Ms. Alfonso, the principal, had visited Mr. Hooker's class and was pleased with his rapport with the children. Parents always praised Mr. Hooker by saying he is much loved and respected, caring, concerned, and interested in the students. She was, however, puzzled by the reading, usage, and grammar scores of the latest achievement tests for his room. The students were not making good progress. Some teachers complained that he bribed the children by giving them high grades. She had spoken to him about his assigning A's and B's to the majority of his students. He replied, "They need positive reinforcement, and I don't feel that they should be marked down for making errors a native English speaker would not make. We need to increase the self-esteem and self-concept of these students." Although Ms. Alfonso was not totally convinced of his argument, she took a wait-and-see approach to the problem. Now it was March and teacher ratings and evaluations were due next month. Ms. Alfonso began to wonder if she were wrong in accepting his view for raising students' self-concept and in ignoring the school's policy that grades reflect performance. Was he emphasizing the affective part of the teaching-learning process at the expense of the cognitive dimension? She began to wonder about what needed to be done to improve this situation.

QUESTIONS FOR DISCUSSION

1. How would you evaluate Mr. Hooker's teaching style utilizing Fiedler's contingency model?
2. What additional information about Mr. Hooker's class would you want to know as his supervisor? What decision-making model could help you obtain and analyze such information? Explain.
3. What supervisory goals and objectives might you want to establish? Would you take a human resources perspective in setting these goals and objectives? Why or why not?
4. How would you enlist Mr. Hooker's support for your supervisory effort? Would application of Hoy and Miskel's decision style model or the authority-freedom continuum suggest how you might garner that support? Explain.
5. What is your personal reaction to Mr. Hooker's educational philosophy?

COMPUTER WARS

The faculty of Franklin Elementary School believes that their principal, Mary Stewart, may be the best principal in the state. She is intelligent, shows consideration to all members of the school community, has a vision of education, and is deeply concerned with the children's development. She also considers staff development important in improving the school culture. Mary has kept up with changes in curriculum and technology. Four years ago she procured thirty-two computers for the computer lab. Each student in the school uses a computer for at least forty minutes a week.

The present system seems to be working well. However, there is a growing vociferous minority of teachers who have requested that the computers be taken out of the lab and two or three be placed in each classroom. These teachers cite articles that claim that computers should be integrated into the regular curriculum and installed in individual classrooms. They have a list of award-winning software designed to be used with computers in the classrooms. Some teachers have plans to buy modems and communication software so they may interact with classes in other schools in citywide and/or nationwide projects.

Most teachers are not computer literate. They are happy to drop their students off at the computer lab, especially on the days that it gives them a preparation period. They cite articles that say computer instruction should be left to a computer expert such as a lab teacher. They claim that important skills such as word processing are best taught in a lab situation.

The principal knows that her faculty is excellent. They are dedicated, caring teachers. They have gone through some tough times together, but this issue is threatening to polarize the faculty. The school budget cannot accommodate both distribution schemes.

QUESTIONS FOR DISCUSSION

1. How much of Mary Stewart's decision will be based on her teachers' expertise and how much on educational philosophy? How could the Hersey-Blanchard leadership model assist the principal in determining what leader style(s) to use in this situation?

2. Under what circumstances should a principal act to resist changes in a school that may be generally viewed as positive for students? Must the (corporate) school culture be considered when taking such action? Why or why not?

3. What are the advantages and disadvantages of storing software such as filmstrips, CD's, audio tapes, and video tapes in either a central area or in the teachers' resource room?

4. What should a principal require of a faculty before new technology is introduced into a school? Does the issue of introducing new technology lend itself to a Quality Circle approach? Why or why not?

THE HUNTER MODEL—YES OR NO?

It was ninety-two degrees when the teachers came into the Crestview Elementary School. Their principal, Tina Kerster, began the first staff meeting of the academic year. The teachers had just negotiated a contract in which they felt they had not received an adequate raise, and the amount of empowerment they had expected was not forthcoming by the school board. One of the critical assumptions teachers had in their efforts to improve schools was to give teachers more control over what they do. Evidently, the school board did not see school improvement through the teachers' eyes.

Tina Kerster had been principal of Crestview for the past eight years. She was respected by the teachers. She stressed academic achievement and supported the staff in their relations with students, parents, and even the central office. She was known to ask teachers for their advice and opinions but always made the final decision.

The beginning of the meeting was similar to other first staff meetings. There was the introduction of new faculty, her pep talk, and some administrative details. Ms. Kerster then began a new topic, the recommendation of the planning committee that had met over the summer to create the goals and objectives for school improvement for the coming school year. The committee consisted of the principal, two teachers, a guidance counselor, the PTA president, and the curriculum director. They had attended a workshop by Madeline Hunter and were impressed by Hunter's application of research for teaching. The committee felt that the steps in a lesson that Hunter proposed could be easily taught to teachers. They believed that most teachers had these behaviors in their repertoire but needed only to become more conscious in using them. The principal had done much reading on the topic and talked with the superintendent about making a commitment for the school to use a Hunter model and become known as a Hunterized school. This commitment would be the staff's development goal for the next two or three years. All teachers would learn and use the Hunter model in their teaching in the next three years. Ms. Kerster further stated that although the school's national standardized achievement test scores were good, they were not excellent. This approach could increase the students' achievement. Though the details had not been worked out, in all probability the evaluation of teachers would be based on the teachers' effective use of the steps in the Hunter model.

As the principal took a breath to go on to another topic, a large number of hands were raised and a barrage of questions were asked. She then spent thirty minutes answering teacher questions that were framed in a manner derogatory or hostile to the Hunter model. During the question and answer period a number of points seemed to come forward. Hunter's steps were indeed based on research and were valid. However, it did not follow that by including these steps in a lesson the effects of each technique would be cumulative. The art, music, and grade levels teachers who taught creative writing said they didn't think a rigid stepwise programmed teaching model would be effective for their students. The new teachers asked if this meant they would have to behave like factory workers and follow a script. Wouldn't the steps decrease their use of professional judgment and personality to enhance learning. Some older teachers voiced the opinion that this was just another fad and the school need not get caught up in it. In a few years it would pass.

The president of the teachers' union said, "This doesn't make educational sense to me. We are being evaluated by a method in which we have had no input."

Another teacher said, "I have just spent the last ten weeks in negotiations. During this time we wanted teachers to have more say in what was happening in our schools. We were unable to get anything in writing but the school board kept saying that they always treated us fairly. They said we could be sure that they would listen to our suggestions and give them a fair hearing. Now they want to make us think and behave like unskilled factory workers while not getting the salary we are worth. I may be forced to teach with this model, but, rest assured, I will volunteer to do nothing extra for the school. I will perform my job in a perfunctory manner as do most workers who are treated as automatons."

The principal who had expected some minor resistance to her proposal, was shocked. The Hunter model seemed so logical to her. It would provide teachers with a common language for talking about teaching, a model from which to derive their teaching techniques, a method for making lesson plans more efficient, and an evaluation system that appeared to be less subjective than the one she was using. Ms. Kerster was greatly disturbed by what had been said.

She dismissed the teachers and went to her office to think about what had occurred. As she left the lunchroom, the principal noticed that many teachers remained at their seats. She wondered what they would talk about.

QUESTIONS FOR DISCUSSION

1. Why were the teachers so opposed to the Hunter model?
2. What should the principal have done to introduce the Hunter model to get better acceptance of it by the teachers?
3. Why do some administrators avoid participative decision making? How could application of the authority-freedom continuum have helped the principal here?
4. Is there any way the principal of an elementary school can provide structures or mechanisms for introducing change into the school? Does the human resources approach to supervision provide a means to the end the principal wants to achieve? Why or why not?
5. How could the Hersey-Blanchard situational leadership model be applied in this instance?

Evaluating Students

ARE WE LOWERING OUR GRADING STANDARDS?

The Kelly School's population had changed from a predominantly middle class to a lower class clientele. The population also consisted of a large number of students enrolled in English as a Second Language classes. The teachers in the upper grades had agreed to a plan of positive reinforcement by using various rewards for good homework and classwork, special recognition for good report card grades, honor badges, and prizes for good behavior inside the classroom.

At report card time, however, 75 percent of Ms. Karnell's students received failing grades. As a result, Ms. Karnell, a sixty-one year old mathematics teacher, was in a difficult conference with the principal. When the principal mentioned the large number of failures she retorted, "These foreign kids have nonschool behavior. Their work is rotten, their attitude is rotten. If I survive the next four years, I will retire. But I will not lower my standards. I am available from 8:30–9:00 A.M. and from 12:30 to 1:00 for special tutoring. None of the students show up. I don't think we do these kids a favor by lowering our standards. They will need to cut the mustard in the world of work. They had better find out what it is really like. All other immigrant groups did it, and I don't see why this group can't.

"I realize that the other teachers think I spoiled the reward system. But I didn't. I gave it integrity. Students who do achieve really deserve the honors. I know the other teachers have put pressure on you to do something, but I think they have lowered their standards."

QUESTIONS FOR DISCUSSION

1. How would you evaluate Ms. Karnell's teaching effectiveness?
2. Do you think she is in harmony with the positive reinforcement approach and has been following that plan in her teaching? Why or why not?
3. What arguments would further support her position? What could you say in criticism of her position? Which is most convincing to you? Why?
4. What does a 75 percent failure rate suggest to you? Would a Quality Circle approach to this problem help alleviate it? Why or why not?

5. How would you respond to her from a human resources perspective?
6. In general, what are your views on student evaluation? What
   type of grading or evaluation system would you favor? What
   decision-making steps would you take to plan, organize, and
   implement a grading system?

A Multicultural Setting

A PRINCIPAL BETRAYED?

John Mills, a white assistant principal in an all-black student elementary school (the enrollment of which is 1800 students), was selected
by the Central Board of Education to become an interim principal
until the Local School Council (LSC) was elected. The eleven members of the LSC consisted of five parents, two faculty members, two
community members, the interim principal, and a nonvoting student.
It was the responsibility of the LSC to select and hire a permanent
principal.

The interim principal supported two black teachers to be members
of the LSC. One of the teachers, Ms. Bovee, was elected. The other
elected teacher, Mr. Franks, was white and a strong union member.
He had filed a grievance against Mr. Mills at one time. The next few
months were a learning experience for all members of the LSC. The
meetings, at time, became chaotic and focused on minor personal
issues. At other times, difficult educational issues such as the following were presented: 1) the setting of standards for teacher performance, 2) the setting of standards for teacher evaluation, 3) the failing
of students who pass the tests but don't do the homework, 4) the
need for a school band program even if it doesn't cost anything, and
5) the large number of students failing sixth grade mathematics.

The principal was not able to provide solutions to these problems
to the satisfaction of the LSC members. Mr. Mills also did not deline-
ate the difficulty inherent in the resolution of these issues. However,
he seemed to be supportive of the parents' positions. The two
teacher members resented this. The teachers were constantly in a
defensive position and always showed the harmful implications of
the LSC's position. As a result, there was a polarization between the
teachers and the parents and concomitant tension between the principal and the two teachers.

Mr. Franks put portions of the State School Code that apply to the
functions of the LSC in the teachers' mailboxes. The principal told
Mr. Franks that he could not distribute this material without his

authorization. The teacher disagreed on the grounds he was providing information about the LSC to his constituents.

Mr. Mills worked on building discipline, bringing order to the school and improving his political base on the LSC. He discovered that race was becoming an issue. He began to deal differently with black and white teachers. He reprimanded white teachers with vigor and turned his back when black teachers committed the same errors (for example, not reporting for lunchroom or recess duty, being tardy to classes, turning reports in late or incorrectly, not having lesson plans for a substitute). This approach caused the morale of the school to plummet.

Meanwhile, Ms. Bovee and the white assistant principal, Mr. Kranski, decided to become candidates for the principalship. Both had prior experience as assistant principals. The LSC decided that the three final applicants for the job were Mr. Mills, Ms. Bovee, and Mr. Kranski. During the interview process, Ms. Bovee dealt with the problem of the poor morale at the school while Mr. Mills ignored the issue. An analysis of the voting showed that the white faculty LSC member cast the deciding vote in favor of Ms. Bovee (who had disqualified herself from the voting because of her candidacy).

Mr. Mills felt betrayed by the faculty. He thought to himself, "I brought order to this school, and to do this I had to hurt some teachers' feelings. Teachers can now begin to function properly."

QUESTIONS FOR DISCUSSION

1. What was Mr. Mill's worst decision? Why? What decision-making step(s) did he avoid or minimize? Explain.
2. How should principals make decisions in a multicultural setting? Is the decision-making process different in a unicultural situation?
3. What could Mr. Mills have done to enhance his position? Could a win/win negotiations strategy have helped him? Why or why not?
4. Is there any process that can decrease the resentment that a faculty member may feel when being disciplined by a principal? Would a human resources perspective by the principal help to decrease any resentment? Why or why not?
5. What is meant by a political base? How does a principal go about building a political base? Is it different from providing quality education to the children? Should the school's (corporate) culture be understood in the building of a political base? Why or why not?

Classroom Management

HELPING AN INEXPERIENCED TEACHER

Roy Larson, a nine year old with a history of being a problem child, has been placed in rooms with "strong teachers" during his first three years. The teachers' discipline methods seemed to keep him subdued, and he met the achievement goals of the school. A staffing on Roy indicated he was not a candidate for special education placement. When pupil assignments for self-contained and heterogenous classes were made for the next year, Roy was again assigned to a strong, experienced teacher. However, during the month of October, Roy's teacher resigned and an inexperienced teacher was hired as a replacement.

Roy immediately took over the class. He made loud noises, threw things, jumped over desks, and fought with other children. He drove the teacher, Susan Stark, to distraction.

Conferences with Mrs. Larson and Mr. Randolph, the principal, did not seem to help. Roy's mother listened and was courteous. She stated that although Roy was a difficult child, the school in the past three years seemed to do a good job with him. "After all, you are the professionals and should be able to deal with tough problems. Isn't that why you get paid?" she said.

"I think he just needs a more experienced teacher who teaches with a stronger hand," the mother said. The principal then mentioned a few counter statements which included parents' responsibilities for the child's education. He also stated that Ms. Stark was a qualified teacher. However, he agreed to think about Mrs. Larson's suggestion.

Mr. Randolph felt Ms. Stark was showing promise as a teacher. He decided to remove Roy from her classroom and transfer him to another room. Thus, he could solve the student problem and give Ms. Stark a better chance to grow as a teacher.

Mrs. Hatter, the other fourth grade teacher, heard through the grapevine of the possibility of Roy's placement in her class. She came into the principal's office and began to object to the idea in a very strenuous manner. "I have my own four discipline problems that are driving me up a wall, and I don't need another difficult child," Mrs. Hatter said. "Ms. Stark is a new teacher. Part of her growth is learning how to deal with problem children. I have enough to do. If you send me another problem, I can't be responsible for what will happen to my class discipline."

Mr. Randolph calmed the angry teacher by saying he was only thinking about the placement. He would consider her feelings in the matter and would talk with her again in a few weeks. In the meantime, would she mind giving Ms. Stark some ideas about coping with Roy?

During the next two weeks, Roy's behavior did not improve. Ms. Stark's class was becoming disorganized. Purposeful instruction was being replaced by a continuous barrage of disciplinary commands. Ms. Stark was becoming more discouraged. Mr. Randolph felt something had to be done, and soon.

QUESTIONS FOR DISCUSSION

1. What essential elements need to be included in a student in-school transfer policy?
2. How might such a policy be developed or revised? Would a Quality Circle approach work in this situation? Why or why not?
3. Do you think the principal was handling the situation in the best way? If no, what other decision-making steps might he have taken?
4. What is your evaluation of the principal's intervention with the parent, Mrs. Larson? Was the principal using the neutral third party conflict management approach here? Why or why not?
5. What might the principal learn from this experience about the culture of his school and "symbolic" management? How might he relate to the culture in Deal and Kennedy's terms in an effort to enhance his leadership and further the educational goals of the school?
6. Miles suggested that one human resources goal is a "cooperative and cohesive work force." What has gone awry in this situation?

"STICKS AND STONES. . ."

Mr. Beeger told Mrs. Campbell, principal of Bruce Elementary School, that his daughter was crying when she came home from school. It appeared that she had been interrupting her fourth grade class. Mr. Linden, the new fourth grade teacher from a closed school in the district, had forced her to lean against sharp pointed wooden stubs that were embedded in a wooden rod. Mr. Beeger said the punishment was barbaric and wanted it stopped. Mrs. Campbell agreed.

Mr. Linden admitted to this unusual type of punishment. He said the class had discussed the matter. The students had voted for the rule that when students became extremely obnoxious, they would be given "the sticks." Mrs. Campbell told Mr. Linden that he could impose other methods of control and punishment, but he had to get rid of "the sticks."

A week later, Mrs. Campbell received two calls. One parent complained that her son had to spend two hours in a large wastebasket. The other child was apparently pushed to the ground by Mr. Linden. The parent claimed the fall caused her child's knee to bleed.

Mr. Linden agreed that John Beck had been placed in the wastepaper basket. He said John only behaved properly when he knew he was going to be humiliated. John was a very arrogant child and needed to be brought down a peg or two. Missy Claypool had been dawdling after the bell rang. "I gave her a push to move her along," Mr. Linden said, "and she fell. I apologized to her. But I also let her know that when the bell rings at recess, she needed to respond to it like all the other children.

"I realize I may be tough on the kids. I expect discipline in my class. In order for children to learn, they need strong leadership. I have been using these methods for twelve years, and they work. In fact, by Christmas time every year, I have students eating out of my hands. They enjoy a strong disciplinarian."

Mrs. Campbell suggested that Mr. Linden meet with her at 11:00 A.M. the next day to discuss in more detail his views of discipline.

QUESTIONS FOR DISCUSSION

1. What do you think of Mr. Linden's approach to student discipline? Does it reflect a human relations or a human resources perspective? Explain.
2. What is your emotional response to his approach, if any? If you had an emotional response and were also principal in the situation, what contingency or situational leadership model could help you deal with this problem rationally? Explain.
3. As his supervisor, what would be the major thrust of your conversation with him? Which conflict-handling style would you choose to apply in this instance? Explain your choice.
4. Would any of Mr. Linden's methods be a violation of state statutes in your state? School policy? Community expectations? Professional ethics? If yes to any of these, how would you present your perceptions to him?
5. If you objected to Mr. Linden's approach, had discussed the matter with him, and he persisted, how would you respond at that point? Would you utilize a win/win or win/lose strategy? Explain your choice.
6. How would you follow up with the parents and the students involved, if at all?

TOO MUCH STRUCTURE?

Mr. Verbat told the principal he had been very excited about his new eighth grade which was composed of the top students. After five years of teaching science to the slow and regular groups, he felt this would be a very interesting year. Mr. Verbat said, "I soon discovered, however, that teaching this group brought new difficult problems. It seems that they have been taught in a very unstructured atmosphere with very little discipline and order."

"I am perhaps somewhat more orderly and rigid than the average teacher, but these students needed to be taught organization and discipline. In the process of establishing my routine and expectations of student behavior, one of the brightest girls in the class, Mary Bock, became a difficult problem for me. She had been talking too much. No matter what I said or did, her talking out loud didn't decrease. She also kept asking me for creative projects rather than the solid, continuous developmental projects I planned for the students."

The principal, Mr. Wilkerson, thought about his response. He pondered Mary's mother's complaint that Mr. Verbat spent too much time on keeping the class quiet, making students form straight lines in the halls, and other classroom management problems. Not enough time was spent on creating challenging work for the advanced group.

Mrs. Bock also complained that Mr. Verbat had been very critical with her daughter, who was beginning to hate science. Unless Mr. Verbat changed what he was doing, Mrs. Bock wanted Mary transferred to a regular class. She would probably learn just as much and, more importantly, would change her negative attitude toward science, according to Mary's mother.

QUESTIONS FOR DISCUSSION

1. Based upon the information provided in this vignette, what is your assessment of the situation?
2. What is the proper response for a principal to make to a complaint from one parent? Which conflict-handling style would be the most appropriate in this instance? Explain.
3. How receptive to supervision is Mr. Verbat? Would either the authority-freedom continuum or the Hoy and Miskel decision styles model be helpful to the principal in deciding how to supervise the teacher? Explain your answer.
4. Again, utilizing the human resources approach, what would be your specific concerns for both Mr. Verbat and the students?

5. How would you express those concerns to Mr. Verbat? Would you schedule a special conference with him or wait until his next regular evaluation session? Explain your choice.

Teacher Ratings

AN ERROR IN TEACHER EVALUATION?

Mrs. Crane was completing her second year as principal of the Jones Elementary School. At the completion of her first year, she gave an efficiency rating of excellent to a majority of teachers. Only a few teachers received a superior rating.

Mrs. Lang, a mature woman who had taught at Jones School for eleven years, strived to be an outstanding teacher. She had always received a superior rating from the previous three principals. Her only excellent rating had come from Mrs. Crane.

Mrs. Lang could understand that one year may have not been enough time to evaluate all the teachers properly. Therefore, she accepted the excellent rating without making any fuss. When she received a similar rating at the completion of the second year, she stormed into the principal's office. She demanded to know the criteria for determining the rating. She was told by the principal that the difference between a superior and excellent teacher was primarily based upon creativity.

Mrs. Lang confronted the principal. She stated that the rating was for efficiency and not for creativity. Mrs. Lang requested that a correction be made because the evaluation was not indicative of the results of her class's standardized achievement tests. Further, creativity was not an acceptable measure of a teacher's work at Jones School. In addition, there appeared to be no reliable and valid measure for a teacher's creativity.

QUESTIONS FOR DISCUSSION

1. What assumptions would you make about the evaluation/supervision process up to this point based on the exchange between Mrs. Lang and Mrs. Crane?
2. What questions would you like to ask both in an effort to test your assumptions?

3. Do you suspect that any elements of sound supervision and evaluation have been violated? Why or why not? If yes, what might they be? If not, what might account for the teacher's reaction?

4. As the principal, would you be willing to modify your evaluation or would you resist changing it? Why? In deciding, would you utilize a decision-making model? If yes, which one? Explain your choice.

5. Which of Likert's Systems most appropriately describes this school? Why?

A SUPERINTENDENT'S REQUEST, A PRINCIPAL'S DILEMMA

Enrollment at the Gens and Evergreen Elementary Schools had decreased by 35 percent. As a result, one physical education teacher had to be assigned only half time to each school. The following year the physical education teacher resigned. A new teacher, Mrs. Shores, was assigned to the two schools. As the year progressed, Mrs. Leon, principal of Gens, discovered that Mrs. Shores was an excellent teacher. She was quite pleased with her performance.

In January, Mr. Prusser, Evergreen's principal, called Mrs. Leon. He said, "I don't think Mrs. Shores is doing her job. She doesn't show enthusiasm, she lacks energy, she is a loner and her classes are too closely structured."

Mrs. Leon said, "I am satisfied with her work. Her attendance is good, and I find her classes well organized. However, I will visit her classes more frequently. Let's talk about this next month."

In February, the two principals' perceptions of Mrs. Shore were still divergent. The superintendent called Mrs. Leon into his office and said, "I have talked with Mr. Prusser, and he won't change his mind about Mrs. Shores. He thinks she smokes pot and is a lesbian. He can't prove it, of course, but he feels his twenty-five years of experience as a school principal have given him certain insights into the problem.

"I depend on my principals for employment recommendations. Since both of you are at an impasse, I am caught in the middle. I would like you, Mrs. Leon, to reconsider your recommendation."

QUESTIONS FOR DISCUSSION

1. As Mrs. Leon, what would be your immediate reaction to the superintendent? What does his request really mean?

2. Upon further reflection, how would you define your responsibility in this situation? Would application of a contingency leadership model be helpful to you here? Why or why not?

3. How would you proceed if Mr. Prusser, the other principal, and his wife were close personal friends of yours? Could Mr. Prusser have fallen into one of the decision traps? If so, which one? Explain.

4. How would you proceed if you knew that Mr. Prusser and the superintendent were regular golfing partners and your relationship with the superintendent was strictly professional?

5. What two or three options, arrived at through a decision-making process, might you suggest to the superintendent?

6. If you were reasonably sure that Mr. Prusser's charges were false, what obligation would you feel to defend the teacher, Mrs. Shores? Why? How far would you go if you did feel that obligation? Would you attempt to apply a win/win or a win/lose strategy in this situation? Explain your choice.

7. Would you feel the same if the charges were true? Does Mrs. Shores have the right to her own personal life?

OBSERVING AND ASSESSING A TEACHER'S PERFORMANCE

During the past summer, Richard Kenetti, principal of Ash Elementary School, attended a two week workshop in clinical supervision. When he returned to school in September he decided to begin observing the teachers more frequently. Mrs. Macy, a second grade teacher, was the first to volunteer to be clinically supervised.

During the preconference, Mr. Kenetti was unsuccessful in getting Mrs. Macy to identify a particular teaching problem. So he suggested that he do a verbatim transcript analysis of her teaching. She agreed and told him to come to observe her class at any time.

A week later Mr. Kenetti observed her lesson in reading and a few minutes of a lesson in mathematics. Upon returning to the office he gave his notes to the secretary to type. Three days later she put the transcript in his in-basket. He was eager to read it but decided he would analyze it at home where there would be no interruptions. That evening he read the transcript.

After reading the transcript he felt very ambivalent about his analysis. He was not sure what he should consider as the basic strengths and weaknesses of the teacher. Furthermore, he wasn't sure how many weaknesses he should identify. After all, a verbatim transcript doesn't reflect the reality of teaching. However, he did feel that by reading the transcript he could better identify and analyze the teaching behavior and that he could identify other behaviors that he had missed while observing.

QUESTIONS FOR DISCUSSION

1. How does the principal decide what patterns or particular teaching events should be identified for analysis and discussion? Would such identification differ if the principal has a human resources or human relations perspective on supervision? Why or why not?
2. Is Mr. Kenetti applying clinical supervision appropriately? Why or why not?
3. How is Mr. Kenetti going to mention any weaknesses he has identified as important if the teacher is not able to identify these same weaknesses? What category of conflict could potentially occur here? Explain.
4. What factors should the principal consider in discussing the work of a teacher? How will the principal know what leadership style to use with this teacher—relations or task oriented?

Teacher Ethics

SLANDER OR MERELY PROFESSIONAL CRITICISM?

Ms. Williams, a sixth grade teacher, had been overheard in the teacher's lounge by Mrs. Creed. Ms. Williams thought Mrs. Creed was a very poor teacher. Whenever Ms. Williams walked by Mrs. Creed's room, her class was noisy. Ms. Williams believed Mrs. Creed tried to be a friend to the children and that they needed a disciplinarian, not a friend.

Later that day, Mrs. Creed confronted Ms. Williams about the critical remarks. Ms. Williams stated, "They are my opinions, and I believe you would become a better teacher if you accepted my criticisms."

A few days later, a parent whose son had shown great academic and behavioral improvement in Mrs. Creed's fifth grade class the previous year asked for a conference with Mrs. Creed. The parent informed Mrs. Creed that Ms. Williams, during parent conferences, told the parents that, although they are up to grade level, the children had not progressed as they should have last year in Mrs. Creed's class. The children were all above average in ability, according to Ms. Williams. The parent stated, "I told Ms. Williams she shouldn't talk like that. I think you are a superior teacher. I thought you should know about this."

Mrs. Creed then sought an appointment to discuss Ms. Williams' behavior with the principal.

QUESTIONS FOR DISCUSSION

1. As principal, how would you respond to Mrs. Creed's concern? Of the several conflict management methods, "linking pin", confrontation, and neutral third party, which would you most likely utilize in this situation? Explain your choice.

2. Would you schedule a meeting between the two teachers? A separate conference with Mrs. Williams? Would you invoke the parent? What decision-making steps would you take in arriving at answers to these questions?

3. What speculation might you make about the relationship between the two teachers? Would an understanding of the school's culture, in Deal and Kennedy's terms, assist you in this speculation? Why or why not?

4. What issues would be addressed by a human resources approach?

MINE OR OURS?

Mr. Kennedy had been teaching seventh and eighth grade science for the last fifteen years at Douglas Elementary School. His cabinets were filled with science demonstration equipment.

A new science teacher, Ms. Jackson, was assigned to the room next to Mr. Kennedy. There was little science equipment in Ms. Jackson's room. She asked Mr. Kennedy to allow her to transfer some of the material to her room. Mr. Kennedy refused. He claimed that he had collected and cataloged the equipment over the years, not only at a considerable investment of his time, but also with his own money. He further stated that he knew where everything was. To distribute it would make his teaching impossible. Mr. Kennedy suggested she begin to collect her own materials. He started with nothing fifteen years ago and built up his collection of materials. Ms. Jackson could do the same.

Ms. Jackson thought Mr. Kennedy unreasonable. The equipment was not his but the school's. It had been purchased with school funds.

Ms. Jackson borrowed the school caretaker's master key and got a copy made at a local hardware store. As the necessity for science equipment occurred, she took what she needed when Mr. Kennedy left the school at the end of the day.

Mr. Kennedy did not notice the missing equipment for several months. In class one day, Ms. Jackson was demonstrating acids and bases with her materials. Mr. Kennedy burst into her room. He accused her of breaking into his cabinet and "stealing" his material in front of Ms. Jackson's students. Mr. Kennedy then left for the principal's office.

QUESTIONS FOR DISCUSSION

1. How would you respond as principal to Mr. Kennedy as he entered your office in a state of agitation and made his complaint?
2. What conflict-handling style would you use, if any, if this was your first year as the principal? If you had been principal for many years? If Mr. Kennedy was an excellent but eccentric teacher? If Mr. Kennedy was a poor teacher, in your opinion, and had received a notice of contemplation of nonrenewal of his contract for the following year?
3. What would you probably do in your initial contact with Ms. Jackson? Would a neutral third party approach work best here? Why or why not?
4. Would you document the incident in either or both personnel files? Why or why not? If yes, what would you record? If you document the incident, would it be an example of a human relations or a human resources approach to supervising personnel? Explain your answer.
5. Would you take disciplinary action against either teacher? Why or why not? If so, what action? Could a staff development program, either group or individual, be helpful in adjusting the behavior and/or attitudes of either or both teachers? Why or why not?
6. Could this incident indicate a problem with the school's (corporate) culture? Why? Would a Quality Circle approach be useful in ameliorating this or similar problems in the school? Why or why not?

References

Keith A. Acheson and Meredith D. Gall, **Techniques in the Clinical Supervision of Teachers: Preservice and Inservice Applications,** 2nd ed. New York: Longman, Inc., 1987).

Anthony J. Cedoline, **Job Burnout in Public Education: Symptoms, Causes, and Survival Skills** (New York: Teachers College Press, 1982).

Rita Dunn and Kenneth J. Dunn, **Administrator's Guide to New Programs for Faculty Management and Evaluation** (West Nyack, N.Y.: Parker Publishing Co., Inc., 1977).

Donald A. Erickson and Theodore L. Reller, Eds., **The Principal in Metropolitan Schools** (Berkeley: McCutchan Publishing Corp., 1979).

William A. Firestone and Bruce L. Wilson, "Using Bureaucratic and Cultural Linkages to Improve Instruction: The Principal's Contribution," **Educational Administration Quarterly 21**, No. 2 (Spring 1985): 7–30.

Carl D. Glickman, **Supervision of Instruction: A Developmental Approach** (Newton, Mass.: Allyn and Bacon, Inc., 1985).

Robert Goldhammer, Robert H. Anderson, and Robert J. Krajewski, **Clinical Supervision: Special Methods for the Supervision of Teachers,** 2nd ed. (New York: Holt, Rinehart, & Winston, 1980).

William Goldstein and Joseph C. DeVita, **Successful School Communications: A Manual for Administrators** (West Nyack, N.Y.: Parker Publishing Co., 1977).

Paula Jorde, **Avoiding Burnout: Strategies for Managing Time, Space, and People in Early Childhood Education** (Washington, D.C.: Acropolis Books Ltd., 1982).

William C. Miller, **The Creative Edge: How to Foster Innovation Where You Work** (Reading, MA: Addison-Wesley, 1986).

Mike M. Milstein, Ed., **Schools, Conflict, and Change** (New York: Teachers College Press, 1980).

Van Cleve Morris, Robert L. Crowson, Cynthia Porter Gehrie, and Emanuel Hurwitz, Jr., **Principals in Action: The Reality of Managing Schools** (Columbus: Charles E. Merrill Publishing Co., 1984).

Thomas J. Sergiovanni and David L. Elliott, **Educational and Organizational Leadership in Elementary Schools** (Englewood Cliffs, N.J.: Prentice-Hall, 1975).

School-Based Management Communication Kit (Arlington, VA: National School Public Relations Association, 1989).

Joseph B. Shedd and Samuel B. Bacharach, **Tangled Hierarchies: Teachers as Professionals and the Management of Schools** (San Francisco: Jossey-Bass, Inc., 1991).

Hersholt C. Waxman and Herbert J. Walberg, **Effective Teaching: Current Research** (Berkeley, CA: McCutcheon Publishing Corporation, 1991).

5

Noninstructional Staff
Relations

The elementary principal should be aware that noninstructional personnel such as custodians, clerks and secretaries, bus drivers, cafeteria workers, and security aides are front line communicators of the school program to the larger community. Noninstructional staff attitudes toward teachers, parents, and students reflect on how noninstructional staff do their jobs and influence the general public. Difficulties with noninstructional personnel are often associated with inadequate job definition, recognition, wages and benefits, improper supervision, dual reporting, local politics, and a failure to socialize them into the espoused values of the school.

Below are questions to assist the reader in resolving the noninstructional personnel problems in this chapter's vignettes.

Do noninstructional personnel know their job descriptions?

Do teachers understand and have accurate expectations for the work of noninstructional personnel?

Has the principal encouraged good mutual relations between the noninstructional and professional personnel staffs?

Do noninstructional persons feel special, cared for, and an important part of the total educational effort?

A SCHOOL SECRETARY FOLLOWS ORDERS

On seeing Ms. Gate walk into the office at 8:15 A.M., Mrs. Mack, the school clerk, asked Ms. Gate to cover a Spanish class first period which began at 8:45 A.M.. Mr. Rodriguez had called and said he would be late. Ms. Gate objected and refused to cover the class because first period is her only preparation time for her science classes which meet in two different rooms. In the past, Ms. Gate had always cooperated, sometimes covering other classes three times a week, but now she said she had some special materials to set up for a demonstration.

Mrs. Mack was adamant. She demanded that Ms. Gate obey her request. At this point, Ms. Gate reminded Mrs. Mack that she was only the school clerk and did not run the school. In addition, Ms. Gate argued that she carried a heavier teaching load than most teachers, and her classrooms are on two different floors.

"You know that the principal has told me to assign teachers to classes in his absence," chided Mrs. Mack. "I've assigned this class to you, and I have witnesses. If you don't take the class," Mrs. Mack screamed, "I'll tell the principal!"

To this outburst, Ms. Gate replied, "I couldn't care less if you had a thousand witnesses. By all means, take this matter to the principal and to the superintendent as well!"

QUESTIONS FOR DISCUSSION

1. In your view, what is the cause of the problem? What category of conflict is reflected here? Explain.
2. As the principal, how would you respond upon hearing Mrs. Mack's complaint? Would an understanding of the school's (corporate) culture assist the principal in responding? Why or why not?
3. Is the assignment of teachers to cover classes, in your view, a proper or wise delegation of responsibility to the school clerk? Why or why not?
4. What might be done to prevent a reoccurrence of the problem?
5. What concerns would you have about the clerk, the teacher, the principal?
6. Does it appear to you that this situation is an instance of unclear policy, inadequate job description, human relations approach, or a human resources approach? Justify your choice.

THE SCHOOL SECRETARY AND OFFICE DECORUM

Jack Collier, principal of Kelley Elementary School, inherited a dedicated professional faculty and Mrs. Katherine Thomas, the school secretary. Mrs. Thomas had been a classroom teacher many years ago before becoming a school secretary. She was now in her fifteenth year at Kelley School. The previous principal was promoted to principal of Kelley School from the teacher ranks and had been good friends with Mrs. Thomas.

Mr. Collier was unhappy with Mrs. Thomas' human relations skills. Her clerical efficiency did not seem to compensate for her loud voice, short temper, resentment to changes in office procedures and teacher communications, and selection of student office help. The school office seemed to always be in turmoil because of some trivial administrative problem. Mr. Collier began to spend more time in the office trying to be a buffer for the minor problems that were developing into major issues because of Mrs. Thomas. When possible, Mr. Collier would sit down with Mrs. Thomas and quietly explain in his dignified manner how she should now deal with certain aspects of her job that day. To each of his suggestions Mrs. Thomas answered, "This is a difficult job and there is a great deal of pressure to get the reports in on time. If the teachers would do their reports correctly the first time and stop interrupting me with unnecessary questions, things would go smoothly. They do not understand the need to meet deadlines, and I have to get after them."

The office climate did not improve. Teachers were constantly making remarks about the office using meteorological terminology (e.g., tempest, hurricane, storm, typhoon, calm). Mr. Collier began to realize that he was spending much more time than he wanted answering clerical questions. Mr. Collier began to weigh Mrs. Thomas' excellent qualifications, clerical skills, and experience against her deficiencies.

QUESTIONS FOR DISCUSSION

1. What factors seem to motivate employees to change? How can an administrator manage those factors to achieve desired performance? Could a contingency approach to leadership assist the principal in solving this personnel problem? Why or why not?
2. At this point, how should Mr. Collier work with Mrs. Thomas? Should Mr. Collier apply a human resources or a human relations perspective to his relationship with Mrs. Thomas? Explain your choice.

3. What do Mrs. Thomas' remarks suggest about her feelings and attitudes about her job? Could she benefit from an individualized staff development program? Why or why not?

4. What nonwork-related issues might be influencing Mrs. Thomas? How does an employer approach those issues with an employee?

5. How would Mrs. Thomas' history at the school influence your decisions? How could an understanding of the school's (corporate) culture help the principal make the appropriate decisions here?

6. As the new principal, what factors would you want to keep in mind about your own role? What category of conflict could materialize in your relationship with the secretary? Explain your choice.

WHAT AM I SUPPOSED TO DO?

Mrs. Lepkow, the principal of Jersey Elementary School, resigned in October because of a severe illness. Mr. Kerr was selected by the Board of Education to replace her on a Monday. On the Friday before he was going to become principal of the school, Mr. Kerr decided to visit with Mr. Traves, the acting principal.

Mr. Kerr parked in the employee lot and noticed the paved hardtop covered with bits of glass, a number of flattened beer cans, and little mounds of dirt. As he entered the building, the door was marked with graffiti and a number of window panes were covered with plywood. The tiled lobby and hall floors appeared dusty and dull, not shiny like his former school. On the way to the school office, he stopped in the boy's washroom and noticed there was no toilet paper in three of the four stalls. Also, one of the supports for the urinals was loose.

On entering the school office, Mr. Kerr heard the school secretary, Miss Stoneheart, respond to a telephone call by saying, "Hello, what do you want? I don't know where he is. You can call back later." When Miss Stoneheart saw Mr. Kerr, she asked, "What do you want?" Mr. Kerr replied, "I would like to see the principal." She said, "He will be back soon. Sit down." While Mr. Kerr waited, he noted that the secretary was abrupt, defensive, and, in some cases, indifferent to students and teachers. When Mr. Traves, the acting principal, returned to the office ten minutes later, Miss Stoneheart said, "There is a man to see you." Mr. Kerr then introduced himself and Mr. Traves stated, "I'm happy to meet you. Let's go into your future office and we can talk." As they entered the office, Mr. Kerr began to wonder how he would deal with the building maintenance and secretarial situations.

QUESTIONS FOR DISCUSSION

1. In general terms, what is your view of how one ought to approach an organization as the new boss?
2. What specific "do's and don'ts" would you suggest in such situations? Should they be guided by a human resources perspective on human nature? Why or why not?
3. What factors do you think might have contributed to the conditions at this school? What decision-making steps would you take to find out?
4. What would you want to know as you formulated your plans before taking over as principal of this school? Who would you want to involve in your information gathering? Would either the Vroom and Yetton or the Hoy and Miskel decision style models help you determine who should be involved? Explain.
5. What would be your first major actions as the new principal? How could those actions be guided by Peters' and Waterman's attributes of successful companies?
6. What would you assume about the culture of Jersey Elementary?
7. Analyze this problem situation utilizing either Likert's Systems or the "maturity" concept from Hersey and Blanchard.

THE CUSTODIAN EVALUATES A TEACHER

Mr. Stephen "Pop" Jones was the custodian and handyman at Adams School for the last thirty-three years. "Pop" got along well with everybody. He did his work efficiently, was always helping teachers and students with projects that required handyman skills, and he even loaned money to the children. Although the school building was thirty-five years old, the grounds looked manicured. "Pop" really knew and did his job. All the faculty loved him, and, at Christmas time, they always bought him a present.

Last year Mr. Wolf retired and a new teacher, Ms. Jens, was assigned to room 105. This room had only 75 percent of the area of the normal size classroom and was called the small room. To compensate for the size, the teacher in this room was actually given a class of no more than twenty students. This year it consisted of the slowest twenty fourth graders.

Ms. Jens had really become enamored with the Piagetian Theory of child development and learning. She decided to do a great deal of hands-on project work and group activities. As the semester progressed, more and more materials were accumulated and makeshift storage cabinets (out of cardboard) were found in every part of the room. To a stranger the room looked chaotic. The principal had received very favorable comments from several parents of the fourth graders about Ms. Jens. She really loved the kids. They never enjoyed school so much and were really learning.

"Pop" made it known, however, that Ms. Jens was a lousy teacher. Her room was always noisy. It was the most disorganized, sloppy, and dirty room he had to clean in the thirty-three years he had been working in the building. Finally "Pop" told Ms. Jens that he could not clean her room because of all the materials on the floor. Ms. Jens said nothing.

The principal, Mr. Phillips, would once a month inspect the rooms for physical plant needs and look at bulletin boards after school. On entering Ms. Jens' room he shook his head. Large paper mache animals were being constructed and the paste was all over the walls, windows and floors. Paper was stuck to the floor, thick dust on the piano, windowsill and chalkboard, boxes were piled upon boxes, and every bit of space covered with children's school work. At the rear of the room was a clothes line on which hung a long large sheet of butcher paper covered with every possible color. The sloppiness of the room disturbed him, and he made a mental note to speak to Ms. Jens in the morning.

QUESTIONS FOR DISCUSSION

1. As principal, what would you say to Ms. Jens? How serious is the problem in your view? What category of conflict is occurring here?
2. If Ms. Jens reported that "Pops" had refused to clean the room, what would be your response? Would you take a neutral third party conflict management stance here? Why or why not?
3. What steps could you take to make this a "win-win" situation?
4. What would be your goals with Ms. Jens? With "Pops"?
5. How would you respond specifically to the comments "Pops" has made about Ms. Jens' teaching ability? What conflict-handling style might you adopt in your responses? Explain your choice.
6. What professional ethics and cultural values concerns would you want to include in your orientation plan for new noninstructional staff? List at least three or four specific issues.

THE STRICT TRANSPORTATION SUPERVISOR

Caleb Fox had been an employee of the Pine Winds Schools for nearly two decades. He started out as a part-time janitor, then became a full-time mechanic, and during the last decade he had been the school district's transportation supervisor. Caleb supervised twenty-five full- and part-time school bus drivers, planned and implemented the many bus routes, and set the rules for both bus driver authority and student conduct on the school buses. He often remarked that his experience as a marine sergeant during the early days of the Vietnam War provided him with the skills he needed to be a supervisor. Caleb was a superb mechanic and repaired all the school district's buses as needed. The school district's pupil transportation safety record was second to none in the state.

The PTO of Bell Elementary School had recently questioned the way in which the rules of pupil conduct on the buses were being enforced by the bus drivers. Mrs. Kingman brought the matter to a head during the last PTO meeting when she complained to other parents that her five year old son had been "kicked off the bus" for a week because he sat in the wrong seat more than two days in a row. Other parents then complained about the excessive punishments their children were experiencing as a result of breaking such rules as "no feet on the bus seats," "no radios on the bus—whether played or not," and "no standing in the aisles or changing seats while the bus was moving."

Bell Elementary School's principal, Sally Farnsworth, read the letter she received from the PTO president asking that enforcement of the rules of conduct on the buses be tempered with reason and understanding of each child's age, physical condition, and social maturity. Ms. Farnsworth knew the bus drivers were merely following Caleb Fox's orders for strict discipline on the buses. Up to now, she had not intervened because of the fine safety record the pupil transportation operation had established over the years. Further, the buses were *always* on time and at their proper locations no matter what the weather or road conditions were. Whenever a bus was needed for a field trip, Caleb never failed to provide a bus and driver, even on "last minute" requests by Ms. Farnsworth's teachers. Therefore, with great reluctance, she asked Caleb to see her about the parents' complaints.

"I'm a busy man, Sally, a very busy man," Caleb impatiently intoned as he entered the principal's office unannounced. Ms. Farnsworth showed him the letter and waited for his response.

"Parents aren't responsible for what happens on the buses, I am," the transportation supervisor angrily charged. "They don't have the foggiest notion of the serious responsibility my bus drivers have for the very lives of their kids. They should be grateful, not critical, of what we do for their kids."

At this point, the principal asked Caleb to sit down. She walked over to her office door and closed it to the outside office area. She then turned to Caleb seated in her guest chair and began to express her thoughts.

QUESTIONS FOR DISCUSSION

1. What category of conflict is exhibited here? Explain your choice. What other potential conflicts are apparent if the identified conflict is not resolved?

2. What should the principal say to the transportation supervisor? What conflict-handling style would work best here? Explain your choice.

3. Can the principal resolve this matter without involving the school district's central office? Why or why not? Could a systems approach to decision making help her decide? Why or why not? Would Hoy and Miskel's expertise-relevancy model be of help to the principal in deciding who to involve? Why or why not?

4. Will a win/win negotiations strategy work in this situation? Why or why not?

5. If Ms. Farnsworth used a contingency approach to leadership in this problem situation, what situational factors or conditions should she consider in determining what leadership style would work here?

6. Is Caleb Fox a task-oriented or relations-oriented supervisor? Explain your choice. Does he reflect Theory X or Theory Y assumptions about human nature? Explain. Would he be responsive to an individualized staff development program? Why or why not?

REFERENCES

William B. Castetter, **The Personnel Function in Educational Administration,** 4th ed. (New York: Macmillan, Inc., 1986).

Edward F. DeRoche, **An Administrator's Guide for Evaluating Programs and Personnel,** 2nd ed. (Boston: Allyn and Bacon, Inc., 1987).

Larry W. Hughes and Gerald C. Ubben, **The Elementary Principal's Handbook: A Guide to Effective Action,** 3rd ed. (Boston: Allyn and Bacon, Inc., 1989).

James M. Kouzes and Barry Z. Posner, "The Credibility Factor: What Followers Expect from Their Leaders," **Management Review** 79 (January, 1990): 29–33.

Standards for School Buses and Operations, Revised ed. (Chicago: National Safety Council, 1985).

CHAPTER

6

Relationships with Pupils

To enjoy the support and confidence of parents, the elementary principal must provide students with an environment for favorable experiences in school. Since most of their school day is spent with teachers, students bring home myriads of information about their teachers and classrooms. When the parent asks, "What did you do in school today?" the principal expects the student's responses to reflect favorably on the school's teachers.

In the education of American children, societal influences may be of hinderance. For example, the problems of racial discrimination and the prevalence of drugs can infiltrate the school. To control these problems, elementary principals need to encourage a philosophy and policies which emphasize the interests of students, teachers, and parents as joint participants in a changing society. Difficulties in controlling the problem areas of our society in the school setting arise because significant values of the participants often are at stake. These values such as freedom of association, right to privacy, and a hedonistic life style can be obstacles to conflict resolution.

Instructional practices may be associated with pupil personnel problems. When written policies do not exist or are unclear or vague in the areas of homework assignments, field trip attendance, grading and reporting systems, the school and its principal are susceptible to student criticism and conflict.

Elementary educators usually show respect for the personal integrity of the student. The student is expected to make some academic and behavior errors in school. In most cases, elementary teachers view student mistakes in an empathetic manner and make suggestions, that is, give guidance and direction for future improvements. In some cases, however, student antisocial behavior requires a severe disciplinary response. Where a handicapping condition is suspected, teachers are required to inform special education professionals so an appropriate assessment can occur. The elementary principal must have enough expertise to know and apply the legal and policy expectations involved in student disciplinary actions and special education placements.

The following questions may help focus the reader on the complications involved in the vignettes in this chapter.

> Are societal dysfunctions such as racial discrimination, drug abuse, and divorce major contributing factors to the conflict?
>
> Is there an issue of fair treatment in the complaint?
>
> Does the school have written criteria for evaluating pupil academic performance?
>
> Is there an adequate policy to help solve the problem?
>
> If no policy exists, should there be one and what should it be?
>
> Should parents and students be involved in making the policy?
>
> Are legal implications included in the resolution of the conflict?

Ethnic and Racial Problems

BOYS IN DISPUTE OR ETHNIC PREJUDICE?

Mrs. Carson, principal at Long School, was surprised to see Mrs. Fellicrow step into the office with a painful expression on her face. It seemed that her son, John, had come home from school with a black eye. John told his mother that Hector Gomez, a safety patrol boy, had beaten him up as he passed the corner on the way home.

Mrs. Carson was surprised to hear this story. She informed Mrs. Fellicrow that Hector was an excellent student. He had never had a discipline problem. However, Mrs. Carson assured Mrs. Fellicrow the boys would be called into the office. She would discover the cause of the fight and appropriate action would be taken.

At 11:00 A.M. the principal called the two boys to the office. Apparently John had been calling Hector a "dirty spic" and other appelations because Hector had "cheated" him out of eight marbles in a marble game. Hector denied he had cheated John. He said his father had told him never to take any derogatory remarks about his ethnicity without fighting back.

QUESTIONS FOR DISCUSSION

1. In situations where the truth may remain unknown, what can be done? In this situation, should the principal use one of the following conflict management methods: "linking pin," confrontation, or neutral third party?
2. What would you tell the two boys? Should you be aware of the decision-making traps as you confer with the boys? Why or why not?
3. What would you report to John's mother? To Hector's parents? Would you play the role of neutral third party with these parents? Why or why not?
4. If you saw this incident as a symptom of an ethnic conflict in the school, what might you do at this point before the problem becomes more serious? What persons in the school and the community would you involve in your efforts? Why? How?

A "LETTER TO THE EDITOR"

Although "The Inquirer" was an elementary school newspaper, the level of its editorials and letters to the newspaper were quite literate. The school newspaper had always been allowed to have a liberal uncensored editorial policy.

As part of a desegregation plan, 60 black students were assigned to the all white 450 student Gordon Elementary School. The white parents in the community had resigned themselves to the plan. A number of Letters to the Editor by white students had been published in the school newspaper, "The Inquirer," suggesting that everyone should make special efforts to make the black students feel welcome.

Later in the year, a "Letter to the Editor" from a white female student was published which criticized the behavior of some of the eighth grade black students. She stated that obscene remarks and lewd suggestions had been made in the school's corridors and lavatories. She no longer felt comfortable walking the school corridors or entering the lavatories. The letter also implied that the black girls would certainly appreciate more appropriate behavior from the black boys.

A few days later, the principal received a signed letter from a number of black parents. The parents resented the implications that the moral character of their children was less than the whites. They demanded a retraction in an editorial and insisted that the faculty sponsor of the paper be changed.

During informal encounters with white parents, the principal was asked about the behavior of the black students. Parents, both black and white, had become upset. The principal sensed that the friendly collegial school climate was changing and not for the better.

QUESTIONS FOR DISCUSSION

1. As the principal, what would be your major concern at this point? Why?
2. How would you respond to the letter and the demands from the black parents?
3. What, if anything, would you do to respond to the concerns of white parents?
4. What, if anything, would you attempt to do with students? Teachers? Community? Central office of the district?
5. How would your approach differ if you had an all-white staff? If you had one black teacher? If it were a blue-collar neighborhood?
6. Does it appear to you that the initial problem was a racial conflict? Why or why not?

Drugs and Disease

A GRADUATION TRIP GOES TO "POT"

The sixty eighth grade students and five teacher chaperones from Courin Elementary School went on the annual graduation trip to the Great Amusement Park in a distant city. There were no apparent problems during the first part of the trip. Everyone was having a good time.

That night in a motel, two teachers discovered that twelve children were "stoned." Upon further investigation, two of the children were found to have pot and cigarette papers on their persons.

The teacher in charge called the principal at home that night. She asked what they, the chaperones, should do next.

QUESTIONS FOR DISCUSSION

1. How would you, as the principal, respond to the call?
2. What decision-making steps would you take if your school did not have a written policy to cover this problem?
3. In your state, would you have any legal obligations in this situation? Would the teachers serving as chaperones? Would you involve law enforcement at this point? Parents?

4. What concerns would remain after the trip, and what would you do about them?
5. In a general sense, what role should the school play in the enforcement of the law? In matters of social and ethical norms which may not be covered by specific law? What would a "moral majority" position be? What would a "civil libertarian" position be?

WE HAVE NOTHING TO FEAR BUT AIDS!

Castle Elementary School is in a blue-collar suburb of a large mid-western city. The school principal, Ms. Gordon, is known as a strong disciplinarian who would support her teachers. She had administered the school for the past twelve years. During the third week of the school year, Mrs. Allen, a parent, came to talk with Ms. Gordon. She told her that her son, who had hemophilia, was infected with the HIV virus. He hadn't been feeling well lately, and she took him to the doctor. The doctor suggested a blood work up since Mrs. Allen's son received several transfusions a few years ago. That was how she found out that her son Larry was infected. Her doctor assured her that a person could contract the virus only by coming into contact with infected blood or by having sexual intercourse with an infected person. She recommended that the principal tell the teachers to wear rubber gloves in case her child Larry began bleeding.

Ms. Gordon thanked Mrs. Allen for telling her and praised her for her concern about not contaminating the other children and teachers. The principal avoided dealing with the inevitable outcome of the infection.

Ms. Gordon immediately called the superintendent to notify him of the issue. The superintendent told her to handle the problem of notifying the school community and to let him know what was going on. The superintendent stated that since she was closest to the community and knew it best, Ms. Gordon should handle the problem. If she needed help, she could call him.

The principal thought over her approach. She decided it would be better to call a teachers' meeting to get the teachers' ideas about dealing with an HIV infected child who was a hemophiliac.

At the meeting Ms. Gordon presented the information to the teachers. She decided not to tell the teachers the infected child's name until the end of the meeting. Ms. Gordon had expected a rational discussion of the problem since so much had been discovered about AIDS in the last five years. After presenting the information she asked for comments and suggestions.

Mary Smith, a third grade teacher, said, "I want to know who this child is. I have some children who fight, scratch, and bite, and I am afraid this behavior could result in the infection of other children. Although I have never been bitten by a third grader, it could happen. I don't think I have the obligation to teach an infected child. A simple nose bleed could infect other students with this virus. After all, dentists and doctors can refuse to treat an AIDS patient."

John, a sixth grade science teacher, said, "I realize the student is innocent but I can't risk getting this disease and giving it to my infant. I recently read that a homosexual dentist with AIDS passed on the virus to a female patient. Perhaps there are mutant viruses that can be transmitted by the breath of an infected person. Although we know a great deal about this virus, much still needs to be discovered. I don't want to take the risk of having the child in my room. After all, we do require the children to take immunization shots for diseases that are not fatal, and, if they don't, we don't allow them to enter school."

Mrs. Smith, a fifty-eight year old second grade teacher, who had a reputation for nurturing the children, spoke next. "AIDS is only transmitted by blood or sex. What you are talking about is pure speculation. I have heard that a person is more likely to get struck by lightning than to be contaminated by everyday living contact with an AIDS victim. After all, there has not been one case of AIDS spreading to other members of a household that includes an AIDS infected child. Our risk is greater to be killed when we drive home than to become infected by an AIDS child. We need to treat this child humanely. To exile the child from school would be cruel. After all, schools are value preference institutions. If we can't behave humanely in a school setting, the larger society can't be expected to either."

Don Stone, a fifth grade teacher replied, "I watch my kids. Those that are in my room and those at home. I try to protect them from things they don't understand. It may be possible that this virus can be transmitted by the drinking water fountain. I don't see how you can be so blasé about this problem. It seems to me we can meet the state requirements for educating this child by homebound instruction. After all, some parents opt for this type of schooling. The rich used to have tutors come to the house to teach their children. I feel sorry for the infected child and the parents, but I don't think we should take any unnecessary risks."

Mary Jones, a sixth grade social science teacher said, "I want to know the name of this child now! After all, he or she may be in my class. Since the school is organized by departments in the three upper grades, the child may make contact with seven different teachers."

Ms. Gordon was stunned. She had always supported her teachers. Her estimate of their feelings was that they would not allow Larry to stay in school. She then told the teachers, "I can't tell you the student's name now. I think it could be considered as an invasion of privacy or a violation of our handicapped law. I will call the school attorney and let you know the name of this child when possible."

The bell rang and the teachers reported to their classes. Ms. Gordon imagined the problems that would arise when the parents found out about this. Did she bungle this problem?

She called the superintendent to report what had occurred. The superintendent said, "I think you will soon hear from some parents. This information will spread like a wildfire. Start getting ready for a community meeting."

QUESTIONS FOR DISCUSSION

1. Should the principal have informed the faculty before the other parents in the school's community? Why or why not?
2. This situation is an example of what category of conflict? What conflict-handling style would be most appropriate for the principal to use?
3. In your state, may a board of education refuse to allow a AIDS-infected child to attend school and, instead, provide housebound instruction? Is an AIDS-infected child considered handicapped under federal and state laws? Why or why not?
4. What decision-making model (steps) would you use if you were confronted with this problem?
5. What should the principal do to prepare for the community meeting? Should she plan on using a win/win negotiations strategy here? Why or why not?

Child Abuse

AN ABUSED OR A CARELESS CHILD?

For the last two months Mrs. Kraus, a fifth grade teacher, observed that Keith's appearance had gradually become dishevelled. Keith seemed to change his gait from week to week. The gym teacher informed her that Keith had a great many bruises on his body. When asked where he got them, Keith answered, "From playing football."

A week later Keith came limping into the classroom. When asked again by Mrs. Kraus what happened, he replied, "I fell down on my way to school." After much persuasion, Keith went to the school nurse who reported that she saw bruises on his back, buttocks, and the backs of his legs.

Mrs. Kraus called Keith's mother. The mother replied that Keith was very accident prone. He bruised easily. Mrs. Kraus was advised not to worry.

A week later Keith came limping into the classroom again. This time he had a black eye. Mrs. Kraus then took him personally to the principal.

QUESTIONS FOR DISCUSSION

1. As the principal, would you be prone to accept the mother's explanation or would you suspect child abuse? Why?
2. If you suspected abuse, how would you proceed using a decision-making model?
3. What is your school policy on reporting child abuse and neglect?
4. What are the reporting requirements and procedures in your state? Who is required to report? When? How? Are there penalties for not reporting? What might make you hesitant to report?
5. What has been your own experience with child abuse and neglect cases in the school setting? Cases involving school personnel?
6. If your teachers appeared to be generally uncertain about how to approach cases of suspected abuse and neglect, what might you do to clarify and assist?

Special Education

THE MEAN PRANK

Mrs. Compton was cleaning up her room on the second floor. It was the last day of school. The students had been dismissed at 10:30. She now had about an hour to secure all her materials for next September and to make sure everything was in the proper place so John, the custodian, could clean her room.

Suddenly four boys with skeleton masks over their faces entered the room. They held water pistols and began to shoot Mrs. Compton in the hair, face, and dress with a green liquid that stained her clothing. In about fifteen seconds, one of the boys said, "Let's go." Although Mrs. Compton was somewhat frightened and outraged, she recognized the voice of Peter Bradford. He was a difficult sixth grader who had been placed in a special education program for next September.

Mrs. Compton dried her face and regained her composure. Then she went downstairs to see the principal, Mrs. Pier.

QUESTIONS FOR DISCUSSION

1. How would you, as Mrs. Pier, respond if Mrs. Compton demanded that Peter be suspended from school next fall? That the school pay for her damaged clothing?
2. What would be your concerns if Mrs. Compton had been the teacher recommending special education placement for Peter and his parents had been very resistant to the placement? What might you do?
3. What would your reaction be if Mrs. Compton wanted you to take no action against Peter and the other boys?
4. What general attitude toward this kind of prank behavior by elementary students makes the most sense to you?
5. What specific responses to student pranks have you found to be very effective? Not effective?
6. In general, what appears to be an appropriate and effective way to gain the cooperation and support of parents in these instances?

SHOULD A HANDICAPPED STUDENT BE SUSPENDED?

Green Elementary School had two Educable Mentally Handicapped (E.M.H.) classes and two Behavior Disorder (B.D.) classes. Ken Kobil, eleven years old, had been placed with Mrs. Rockwell, a B.D. teacher, for three months. He had been placed in the B.D. program because of a long history of behavior problems and his learning disability. Ken was often truant. When in school, he was continuously disruptive which resulted in six disciplinary conferences in the last two months.

The principal, Mr. Pouch, received a note from Mrs. Rockwell, "Come to my room immediately! Help!" When the principal entered the room, he saw James Lincoln lying on the floor, moaning, holding his jaw. Blood was coming out of his mouth. Mrs. Rockwell said that Ken had hit him with a hard object, a bronze statuette, across the mouth. She insisted that James' mother be called to take him to a hospital, doctor, or dentist and that Ken be suspended and sent home immediately.

While walking down the stairs with the reluctant Ken, Mr. Pouch thought of what he would say to James' mother. She had been against her son's placement in the self-contained B.D. class to begin with but was convinced by him that the placement would help Jim's educational and social development. Public Law 94-142 ran through his mind. Can a B.D. child be suspended for this behavior? After all, isn't that why he was assigned to this class?

QUESTIONS FOR DISCUSSION

1. What is your understanding of PL94-142 in this regard? If unsure, how would you clarify the question?
2. What would you say to James' mother? What conflict-handling style should you be ready to use in your discussion with the mother? Explain your choice.
3. What would you do with Ken? With his parents? What decision-making steps would you take in determining what to do?
4. If you disagreed with the teacher, how would you counter her seemingly strong feelings? Would you apply a win/win or a win/lose negotiations strategy? Explain your choice.
5. IF Ken's Individualized Education Program (IEP) seemed to be in serious question in your mind, what would you do? What alternatives would you consider?
6. What if none of the alternatives appeared appropriate? Or were very costly? Would a human resources perspective help the principal in a situation like this? Why or why not?

A DIFFICULT CHILD, A PROBLEM MOTHER

The principal, Mrs. Dulley, had called in Mrs. Johnson, a sixth grade teacher, to have a conference about a transfer student. Mrs. Johnson began by saying, "I was having problems with James Corley. His behavior was exceptionally methodical, yet his performance was so poor that I felt he belonged in a lower grade. In checking James' records, I discovered that he had a normal score on a group IQ test and had missed four months of school last year because of serious injuries suffered in an auto accident.

"I sent for Mrs. Corley, and she confirmed that James had missed much school. However, the Corleys' doctor had said he was completely healed. Mrs. Corley said he was a little spoiled by the attention given him while recovering from the accident. I said James should be placed in the fifth grade where he could make up the work he missed. He could then compete with children at his level and be more at ease. James' mother felt this would not be psychologically right for him at this time.

"James earned all F's on his first report card. I held another conference with Mrs. Corley. But she said I was pressuring her son and causing a setback to his emotional recovery. The conference didn't go well at all. Neither of us felt that something positive was going to happen next.

"James' school work was so poor that I recommended he be tested by a psychologist. His mother agreed. As you know, the results showed his verbal IQ to be 68. But James' mother wouldn't approve of a full case study. I think he should be placed in the E.M.H. program.

"What do you think, Mrs. Dulley?"

QUESTIONS FOR DISCUSSION

1. What information would you want to have in making an assessment of a student? Did Mrs. Johnson present you with adequate information? Should you be cognizant of the decision traps here? Why or why not?
2. To what would you attribute the mother's unwillingness to approve a full case study? What might you do in response to your guess about that, if anything?
3. What procedures would be involved in making an Educable Mentally Handicapped placement?
4. Using a contingency leadership model approach, what situational factors should you consider before you decide what leadership style is most appropriate here?
5. If you have had some experience with similar cases, what have you found to be the most difficult aspects of such cases? If you have not had that experience, what might you guess to be difficulties? What strategies or procedures seem to be helpful?

Instruction

TOO MUCH HOMEWORK?

Mrs. Ruth, principal of Casey Elementary School, was inspecting the report cards before they were sent home in two days. She felt this was a necessary supervisory task and allowed her to be aware of honor roll and failing students and grade distributions of classes. The comparisons of the grades for the last three years indicated there was a general grade deflation. Mrs. Ruth began to wonder about its cause.

Mrs. Ruth had put the records and data sheets away when Mrs. Gold, Billy's mother, came into the office for a 2:00 P.M. appointment. "I don't know what is happening Mrs. Ruth," she said, "but my son is either getting dumber or your teachers are becoming slave drivers. Billy has been on the honor roll for the last five years. However, for the past two years he spends three hours a day on homework. Now this term he is even studying on weekends. I don't mind high standards, but the amount of homework has become unreasonable. I talked with his teachers. They say the accountability aspects of the curriculum and the strict guidelines of the district are responsible for the increase in homework. One teacher whom I have known for a long time also told me that the administration is always looking at the standardized test scores. The scores are used as a club over the teachers. Mrs. Ruth, I don't know what you can do about it, but the students and teachers are becoming nervous wrecks."

QUESTIONS FOR DISCUSSION

1. How would you interpret the apparent grade deflation? Would you view it as a positive or negative sign?
2. How could Lipham's decision-making model help you determine if Mrs. Gold's reading of the teachers' sentiments was accurate or not? Would a "linking pin" be useful in this situation? Why or why not?
3. What would you do if you supported the policy of strict accountability and attention to standardized scores? If you did not?
4. Would you wonder if other parents might share Mrs. Gold's view? If so, how might you find out for yourself? Would site-based management be useful in helping the principal assess parent/community feelings here? Why or why not?
5. If Mrs. Gold is correct, which of Likert's Systems would best fit this school and its district? What would that mean?
6. How does grade deflation reflect the culture of the school? How might the principal's understanding of the culture assist her in managing the problem?

THE SUPERINTENDENT GIVES AN ASSIGNMENT

Lincoln Elementary School is located in a small working-class suburban community. It is in a unit (K-12) district. The high school students attended a centrally located high school. Follow-up studies indicated that the majority of the high school students majored in the vocational subjects rather than in areas that required higher education after high school. The studies also indicated that the dropout rate has been exceedingly high for the past three years. Attendance for the Lincoln School had also dropped and was now approximately 85 percent. Reading scores were below national norms across the district. There was an atmosphere of discontent regarding student performance in the basics among the parents and community.

The superintendent called a meeting of the principals and provided more discouraging details about the school district's student problems. The superintendent asked each principal to prepare a set of objectives for improving his/her school's student personnel policies and to form a committee composed of representatives from students, parents, and faculty. The purpose of the committee is to make school improvement recommendations relative to student personnel.

Mr. Church, Lincoln's principal, returned to Lincoln School after the meeting. After the school closed for the day, the principal poured himself a cup of coffee, got some paper and pens, and began to outline his thoughts.

QUESTIONS FOR DISCUSSION

1. As Mr. Church, what thoughts come to your mind?
2. What factors might account for the student profile indicated here?
3. How would you select persons for the committee? What criteria would you use for membership? Would Vroom and Yetton's decision styles model be useful to you in the selection process? Why or why not?
4. How would you prepare the set of objectives? How does the development of the objectives relate to the work of the committee? Would a Quality Circle approach work in this instance? Why or why not?
5. What additional information might be useful to your task and the work of the committee? How could that information be obtained and by whom? Would site-based management be likely to facilitate the search for more information here? Why or why not?
6. What other theories or research findings might be helpful in your effort to carry out the superintendent's request?

EVALUATING THE WHOLE CHILD

"Mr. Tait is here for his appointment," the secretary said over the intercom. "Fine. Send him in," replied the principal, Mr. Gault.

"Come in and sit down. How are things in the fifth grade?"

Mr. Tait replied, "Everything is going along reasonably well, but I have a particular problem with Ben Bright. As you know, he is a very able fifth grader. His reading and arithmetic scores are well above average. However, he turns in no homework, does very few assignments, and never pays attention or contributes to the class discussion. He is becoming the class clown, and, in general, he is very immature. The few enrichment assignments I gave him were started with a burst of enthusiasm, but, in a short time, he lost interest. Nothing is ever complete." Mr. Tait further lamented, "I really don't know what to do with him. I failed him the last marking period and notified his parents of the problem. They were not too concerned but agreed that maybe the failing grades would motivate him to do better in class. They were very adamant, however, in stating that he should not be retained for next year. They stated that education should be based only upon academic achievement as measured by achievement tests." Mr. Tait sighed, "I just listened to Ben's mother and didn't reply.

"My own philosophy of education goes beyond achievement tests," Mr. Tait said. "Grading should include a host of other variables such as following directions, complying with assignments inside and outside of school, cooperation, initiative, and, in general, doing that which is required. These traits are as important as test scores in adult life." Mr. Tait then firmly stated, "Unless Ben improves, I am going to fail him at the end of the year.

"The reason I am here," Mr. Tait intoned, "is I want you to be aware of the possible problem with his parents." Mr. Gault sat back in his chair and began to think of his reply to Mr. Tait.

QUESTIONS FOR DISCUSSION

1. Do you agree with Mr. Tait's philosophy? Why or why not? How would your own views influence your response to him? To what extent does the authority-freedom continuum apply here?

2. What school policy might apply and how? How might the principal's understanding of the school's (corporate) culture assist him in responding to the teacher?

3. Do you think Mr. Tait wants anything more from Mr. Gault other than informing him about the problem? Why or why not? If Mr. Tait wants something more, what is your hunch and how would you act on that hunch?

4. What would be your concerns for the student? What might account for his working below his ability level? What suggestions might you give Mr. Tait to enhance his instruction with this student?

5. What concerns would you have for the student's parents? What suggestions might you give Mr. Tait in his work with the parents? Would you, as principal, adopt a neutral third party conflict-management approach here? Why or why not?

THE DUNCE CAP REINCARNATED

Lawrence is a small emotionally and socially immature boy in the seventh grade. Mrs. Smith had read in his anecdotal file that he had been a behavior problem to all his former teachers. In class he was always talking out and moving about the room. When reprimanded, he became hostile and belligerent. Mrs. Smith had tried many methods to control his behavior. Nothing seemed to work.

During lunch, while discussing Lawrence with other colleagues, Mrs. Smith was told about a method a teacher in another district used to control a child.

When Mrs. Smith returned to her seventh grade class that afternoon, she discussed the problem of talking out and disturbing the class and its effects on the classroom learning. She suggested that any student who talked out of turn too frequently would be required to wear a large red tongue made from construction paper which would be pinned on the offender's chest. The students voted for this punishment unanimously.

That same afternoon, Lawrence was worse than usual. His talking out finally reached the point where Mrs. Smith said, "I've had it."

Mrs. Smith cut the tongue from red construction paper and, in front of the class, she pinned the tongue on Lawrence's shirt. Lawrence ripped it off. She repeated the act. Lawrence tore it off again. He screamed that if she tried to do it again, he would hit her.

Mrs. Smith wasn't going to be threatened by a student in front of her seventh graders. She started to pin the tongue again. Lawrence hit her in the chest. Mrs. Smith immediately retaliated by giving him a smack across the mouth. She then sent a student for the principal.

QUESTIONS FOR DISCUSSION

1. As the principal, what is the first thing you would do upon entering the classroom? Upon entering, what category of conflict would you see? Explain.

2. What would be your thoughts as you became more aware of what had happened, and what would be your immediate concerns? In responding, what conflict-handling style would you use, if any? Explain your choice.

3. Would you take a human resources or a human relations perspective in deciding what to do with the *student* who struck the teacher? Explain the perspective you would take. What school policies might apply?

4. Would you take a human resources or a human relations perspective in deciding what to do with the *teacher* who struck back? Explain. What school policies might apply?

5. What is your assessment of how Mrs. Smith, the teacher, handled the situation? How would you communicate your concerns to her, and how would you follow-up in an effort to prevent future problems of a similar nature?

6. Would you notify the student's parents, and if so, what would you tell them?

7. What concerns would you have for the other students in Mrs. Smith's class, and how would you act on those concerns?

SAFETY FIRST?

Mr. Wallace, the physical education teacher, began an explanation of his problem with Patricia Dowd, a student in his gym class. "Gymnastics for elementary school children is fun; it builds strength, increases flexibility and agility, and develops confidence. I remember when Patricia was in fourth grade. She was afraid to do a somersault. With some effort she finally learned how to do it. Each year, according to our curriculum guides, we progress into more difficult activities. Pat has been making progress albeit slowly.

"She came to us with a note from her father that stated that he wanted Pat excused from gym until the classes on gymnastics were over. He said she has always been a clumsy and fearful girl in sports and can see no value in gymnastics. Besides, he heard of a student being in a hospital for six months because of gymnastics stunts. In addition, he says he is a lawyer and will get a court order to stop us from forcing Pat to participate or for penalizing her for not participating. I don't see how we can have a continuous developmental program. We would not allow a student to be excused from mathematics because a parent thought the material too difficult for his child."

The principal replied, "Mr. Wallace, please give me the note, and I will get back to you later."

QUESTIONS FOR DISCUSSION

1. What category of conflict is reflected here? Explain your choice. Framing the conflict in terms of "rights," what rights are involved for the student, the parent, the school, and how does one weigh them in the balance?
2. Would you approach the father with a win/win negotiations strategy or a win/lose strategy? Explain your choice.
3. As a school administrator, what are your first inclinations and feelings when threatened with legal action? What might be some reasons behind your immediate responses? What steps would be helpful for you to take when confronted with legal threats?
4. Moving beyond concern for rights, what relationship and educational concerns would you have in this instance regarding both teacher and student?

I WANT ALAN TO GO TO WASHINGTON

The principal, Mr. Dugham, received a phone call from Mr. Peterson, parent of Alan, an eighth grade boy. Mr. Peterson complained that his son would not be allowed to go on the graduation trip to Washington during the spring holiday. Mr. Daidalus, who was in charge of the trip, screened the applicants and declared that Alan was a discipline problem. Alan was always creating problems for other students. Mr. Daidalus also was afraid that Alan would cause severe disruptions on the trip. Mr. Peterson stated that because of his son's difficult adjustment to school, he needed to feel part of his class. He thought that this trip could help him because it was not in an academic environment.

QUESTIONS FOR DISCUSSION

1. As principal, where does your primary loyalty lie, with students, teachers, parents, elsewhere? Why and how do you decide? Would application of a contingency leadership model assist you in deciding? Why or why not?
2. How would you respond to the parent if you knew Alan and agreed with the teacher's decision? If you knew Alan and disagreed with the teacher's decision? If you did not know Alan?
3. Would a school policy apply in this case? If so, would you adhere to it? Why or why not?
4. Would you respond differently if Alan's father was a member of the school board? If he was a prominent professional in the community? If he was a blue-collar worker, uninvolved in the community, and had frequently called to criticize the school?
5. What are your personal views on how closely tied participation in extracurricular activities ought to be to academic performance? How are those personal views conditioned by a human resources or human relations perspective on human nature?

EXACTING IS DETRACTING

Mrs. Hutton, Jeffrey's mother, entered Principal Sweet's office ready to fight. After quickly saying hello, she sat down and took out a mathematics test that still showed eight creases on it. Mr. Claudio, the fourth grade teacher, had his students do this so each arithmetic problem was solved in each section of the "8 1/2 x 11" notebook page.

"I don't understand this. Jeffrey is a superior student. On his third grade achievement test, he scored at the 6.0 level. He has always received A's in arithmetic. Now Mr. Sweet, I want you to look at this paper. Mr. Claudio took off eight points for an incorrect heading, fifteen points for Jeffrey not showing his work which he did in his head, twelve points because the seven looks like a one, and six points because he went outside the boxes on three problems. From a paper that should be a hundred, Jeffrey scored 59, a failing grade. It seems to me that the teacher should be grading the students on arithmetic achievement and not neatness, heading, and handwriting." Mrs. Hutton continued, "I talked with Mr. Claudio, but he says we need to teach students how to organize, be neat, and follow directions. He says he already had warned Jeffrey he would take off points on his homework assignments. Jeffrey has refused to change his bad habits. Unless he stops penalizing Jeffrey for his poor habits, he will continue to turn in sloppy work. These poor habits will become even worse." Mrs. Hutton further complained, "I don't agree with this. What counts in arithmetic is the correct answer. I want this failing grade changed to an A which Jeffrey deserves."

QUESTIONS FOR DISCUSSION

1. What are your speculations about the student-teacher relationship in this case? Does the teacher reflect Theory X or Theory Y assumptions on human nature? Explain.
2. Do you agree with the teacher's instructional methods? If yes, how would you interpret such agreement to the parent? If you do not agree, what then?
3. In your view, can or should a principal ever override a grade given by a teacher? What school policy would apply? What policy would you favor for disputed grades? Explain your justification.
4. What other concerns would you have in this situation? Would any or all of Peters and Waterman's attributes of successful companies apply to the teacher's methods in this situation? The student and his work? Explain.
5. How do you usually respond when people make demands to you? What approach would appear to work well when you are confronted with a demand?
6. Apply the human resources perspective to this problem situation.

Tragic Event

TRAUMA AT ELM ELEMENTARY SCHOOL

Frank Williams, principal of Elm Elementary School, answered his telephone at 10:30 A.M. A woman who identified herself as a reporter for the local neighborhood paper said, "Mr. Williams, I want to inform you that a student of yours and her parents were brutally murdered sometime during the night. The bodies of Mr. and Mrs. Gene

Tacco, their 11 year old daughter, Barbara, and their three year old son, Allan, were all found with their throats slashed at 9:45 this morning. Could you tell me something about Barbara and her parents?"

This information hit Mr. Williams like a thunderbolt. He replied, "I am really too disturbed to make any comments about the Tacco family at the present time. Could you call me back in half an hour and I will be in a better state of mind to talk to you." He then called the police department to verify what the woman had said. The desk sergeant said there were four homicides at 612 Chase Street, the Tacco family's address.

The principal began to think about Barbara. She was in sixth grade, had been a good student, and sang in the school chorus. A model student. He had met her parents a few times. They seemed cordial and were proud of their daughter. He wondered how the staff and the rest of the students would react to the brutal murder in the community. He thought about the teachers and students who knew Barbara since first grade. He knew that today he would have to help the school community deal with this tragedy. It would be a very emotional and unusual day.

Elm Elementary School is in a typical middle class community. Its curriculum was oriented toward academics and the teachers and parents stressed high standards. Murders of this kind did not happen in Platsville, and Mr. Williams wondered if there would be more emphasis placed on school security. This kind of trauma was not ever considered.

The principal began to think how he should handle this tragic news. Who should he contact first, the counselor, the homeroom teacher, or the superintendent? What other steps did he need to take to help the school deal with the tragedy?

QUESTIONS FOR DISCUSSION

1. Who should the principal contact first when there is an impending crisis of this nature? Why? What decision-making steps should he take here?
2. Should the principal talk to the reporter? Why or why not? If yes, what should he say?
3. Can you think of any procedures, policies, or guidelines that can help the principal deal with this problem?
4. Suppose the principal had been informed that Barbara had committed suicide. Would the same guidelines you provided for the question above be applicable?
5. Could the Vroom-Yetton decision styles model help the principal decide how to involve others? Why or why not?
6. Is this situation conducive to a Quality Circle approach? Why or why not?

REFERENCES

Kern Alexander and M. David Alexander, **American Public School Law,** 2nd ed. (St. Paul: West Publishing Co., 1985).

Arthur Blumberg and William Greenfield, **The Effective Principal: Perspectives on School Leadership,** 2nd. ed. (Boston: Allyn & Bacon, Inc. 1986).

William M. Bridgeland and Edward A. Duane, eds., **Elementary Schools and Child Abuse Prevention** (Newbury Park, CA: Corwin Press/SAGE Publications, 1990).

Leonard S. Cahen, Nikola Filby, Gail McCutcheon, and Diane W. Kyle, **Class Size and Instruction** (New York: Longman, 1983).

Carolyn M. Evertson, Edmund T. Emmer, Barbara S. Clements, Julie P. Sanford, and Murray E. Worsham, **Classroom Management for Elementary Teachers** (Englewood Cliffs, N.J.: Prentice-Hall, 1984).

Richard A. Gorton and Gail T. Schneider, **School-Based Leadership: Challenges and Opportunities,** 3rd ed. (Dubuque, IA: Wm. C. Brown Publishers, 1991).

Eugene R. Howard, **School Discipline Desk Book** (West Nyack, N.Y.: Parker Publishing Co., 1978).

Vernon F. Jones and Louise S. Jones **Comprehensive Classroom Management: Motivating and Managing Students,** 3rd ed. (Boston: Allyn & Bacon, Inc., 1989).

Mary Margaret Kerr and C. Michael Nelson, **Strategies for Managing Behavior Problems In the Classroom** (Columbus: Charles E. Merrill Publishing Co., 1983).

C. LaMar Mayer, **Educational Administration and Special Education: A Handbook for Administrators** (Boston: Allyn & Bacon, Inc., 1982).

Jacqueline K. Minor and Vern B. Minor, **Risk Management in Schools: A Guide to Minimizing Liability** (Newbury Park, CA: Corwin Press, Inc., 1991).

School-Based Management: A Strategy for Better Learning (Arlington, VA: American Association of School Administrators, 1988).

Charles H. Wolfgang and Carl D. Glickman, **Solving Discipline Problems: Strategies for Classroom Teachers,** 2nd ed. (Boston: Allyn and Bacon, Inc., 1986).

CHAPTER

7

School-Community
Relations

The population in many school districts may not be familiar with the tasks of education and understand how the schools attempt to achieve their mission. Although educators believe that many of their problems could be solved if there were only enough financial support, the elementary principal is confronted with many problems and parental requests that are nonfinancial. Since state statutes assume a working relationship between the school and community, the principal should know how to develop procedures and programs that foster school-community compliance with state and local educational mandates.

A marked departure from the customs and traditions of a community or a school may meet resistance. Time and effort are needed for an innovation to be accepted. In our rapidly changing society, social inventions are created at a fast pace and affect the schools. Issues regarding religion, desegregation, academic freedom, censorship, and curriculum changes appear regularly, but each community is not homogeneous in its opinion of how the issues should be resolved. When an issue has been resolved and board of education policy is established, the principal must use his or her administrative decision-making knowledge and skills within a perspective of contingency leadership to implement the policy.

Many of the vignettes in this chapter deal with issues which have not been decided by either law or school district policy. The subpublic which parents may represent has certain expectations, needs, or philosophy that puts pressure on the school to modify its goals, procedures, and/or standards. In some cases, the pressure for change may even be a threat to the existing impartiality of the school. The special interests of parents or pressure groups foster biases that are at the same time supportive and inimical to the development of democratic values. The principal should take the criticism or demands and use them to strengthen existing democratic values or develop constructive practices or goals for the school.

A number of general questions can be asked when studying the school-community vignettes:

Is there a legitimate basis for community demands?

How do they affect the school?

The community itself?

Is the integrity of a professional in the school being challenged?

How can an illogical or unacceptable demand be turned to a legitimate request?

Is the request of such a nature that it needs to be communicated to the various subpublics of the community?

Is a new board policy or school practice required to meet the parental request?

Professional Discretion

THE DICTIONARY IS DIRTY

The secretary to Ms. Sato, the principal of Green Elementary School, knocked on the door and said three parents were here to see her about a very important problem. She told the secretary to bring in the parents. The serious manner in which they entered caused Ms. Sato to become somewhat tense. Her sensitivity increased considerably.

Mrs. Prudy, one of the parents, said they had read an article about the Education Commissioner in another state banning certain textbooks. In their examination of their children's texts, they found that the Webster's New World Dictionary of the American Language had objectionable entries. They then gave Ms. Sato the following list:

1. bed—p. 81 to have sexual intercourse with
2. fag—p. 341 a male homosexual
3. horny—p. 459 sexually excited

4. hot—p. 460 having strong sexual desire—lustful
5. knock—p. 529 to make pregnant
6. queer—p. 785 homosexual
7. rubber—p. 838 condom
8. shack—p. 881 shack up with—to share living quarters with (one's lover)
9. slut—p. 908 sexually immoral woman

Ms. Sato looked up in astonishment after reading the list of objectionable entries in the dictionary. Mrs. Caputo, another parent, said "It seems to us that this language is blatantly offensive and could cause embarrassing situations in the classroom. Many of these words are not found in the newspaper. We want these words to be inked out of the dictionary or else new dictionaries purchased."

Mrs. Melville added, "We know there has been talk at this school to introduce a sex course. We are opposed to it. It is the family's business to teach students about sex. Certainly schools can't do it. Look at the increase in the number of illegitimate births."

Certain thoughts ran through the astonished mind of the principal. Indeed they have been talking about a family education course. They had two pregnancies in the upper grades. Is there an issue of academic freedom here? Teacher morale? Orthodoxy? Laughing stock in the state? Integrity?

Ms. Sato asked if anyone wanted a cup of coffee and proceeded to reply to the parents' concerns.

QUESTIONS FOR DISCUSSION

1. Would you censure the dictionary?
2. Utilizing the Conflict-Handling Styles format (Figure 1.1), which style would you apply in this situation? Why?
3. Is the problem in this vignette a substantive one only, an affective one only, or a substantive and affective conflict? Why do you think so?
4. How would you proceed if you were Ms. Sato? Which decision-making model would seem most appropriate? Why?
5. Can a human resources approach apply to individuals or groups outside the school? Explain.

TEACHERS' PERSONAL FREEDOM JEOPARDIZED

Mrs. Yule, principal of McCalley Elementary School, skimmed the Saturday newspaper. She noticed a story on the third page about a group protesting against the use of nuclear reactors for energy. As she read the story, the names of those arrested included two of McCalley's teachers—Bill Williams, a fourth grade teacher, and Jane Beck, a second grade teacher. Bill was a tenured teacher with six years experience, and Jane was in her second year and up for tenure. The newspaper listed Bill and Jane as residing at the same address. Both teachers had taken Friday as a personal business day.

Monday morning found Mrs. Yule meeting with parent representatives who had a petition with 100 signatures requesting the firing of the two teachers. Accompanying the parents was the minister of the local church.

QUESTIONS FOR DISCUSSION

1. What is the first thing you would do in Mrs. Yule's position? Why?
2. What are the issues and values presented by this vignette? List at least three.
3. How would a systems approach to decision making operate in this instance?
4. How far ought the school intrude into the private lives of teachers, and what level of personal conduct is a reasonable expectation by the school system? How does the administrator make those decisions?
5. What if some of the school's (corporate) values conflict with those of the community?
6. What if some of the school staff's values conflict with those of the community?

A TEACHER SPEAKS HIS MIND ON DRUGS

Mr. James, an eighth grade social studies teacher, was invited to a local discussion group. He volunteered to be part of a panel discussion at the next meeting which had as its title, "What Can Schools Do About Student Drug Abuse?" At the meeting, he presented a rather controversial position on the use of drugs. He stated that parents use drugs; that society is very drug-oriented; and that children emulate parents and other adults. In addition, children are growing up and experimenting with various aspects of our culture. He further stated that marijuana and cocaine are not narcotics and should be legalized, not just decriminalized as done in some states. Nonnarcotic substances like marijuana are not as harmful as tobacco or alcohol. Also, Mr. James felt that children under sixteen, particularly those in elementary schools, should not be suspended from school because of their use of marijuana. If they are going to be able to learn to use drugs properly, they need guidance that is not punitive.

Mr. James' comments were reported to the local press. A day later, the president and other officers of the P.T.A. came to the principal's office to ask what the principal was going to do about Mr. James.

QUESTIONS FOR DISCUSSION

1. Is Mr. James faced with a role conflict? If yes, explain the nature of that conflict. If no, explain why not.
2. What additional information might the principal want to know, if any?
3. What might Mr. James have done prior to this incident to prevent this problem from developing?
4. Would confrontation techniques be appropriate in this instance? Why or why not?
5. Would it make any difference if Mr. James had stated at the beginning of his remarks that he did not speak for the school district or as a teacher but was stating his own personal views on the subject? Explain.

A SCHOOL-BUSINESS PARTNERSHIP?

Alice Hammersmith, the school district's dietician, was already waiting for Jack Sinn, Craig Elementary School principal, when he arrived at the school on Monday morning. "Jack, I need to see you right away," Alice emphatically said. " Why, come right in," Mr. Sinn said as he pointed toward his office.

Without waiting to sit down in Mr. Sinn's guest chair, Ms. Hammersmith pointedly accused Mr. Sinn of bypassing her office while working on an initial agreement with McClarence's Fast Foods for testing various fast foods with Craig School's pupils. "What's this I hear and read in the local media about your negotiations with McClarence's to have our pupils act as guinea pigs for its experimentation with different fast foods?" Ms. Hammersmith chided.

"Alice, we haven't cut a deal yet, we're just talking about possibilities," Mr. Sinn said defensively. "I got the okay from the superintendent to start talks with McClarence's," the principal asserted.

"Do you realize what you're playing with here, Jack? The health of our pupils, that's what," the dietician vehemently countered. "When it comes to food and nutrition in this district, I am the accountable supervisor. I must be involved in these matters even at the start."

"I'm sorry Alice, but I don't think it is necessary for you to be involved at this stage," Mr. Sinn countered. "When an agreement is made you certainly would be asked to monitor the conditions of that agreement. The school stands to gain immensely from the proposed partnership here. McClarence's is prepared to underwrite all the hardware for an ultramodern twenty station computer lab in Craig Elementary School. Further, pupils would be asked to pay only for the cost of the food McClarence's would provide—no additional costs for preparation, personnel, packaging, etc. It's a testing program to see what quick preparation foods kids will eat at lunch time in an elementary school. Also, our own food service personnel would continue to prepare and serve the food under the supervision of a McClarence's manager."

Flabbergasted, Ms. Hammersmith refuted Mr. Sinn's claims by saying, "Do you have any idea of the nutritional value of fast foods and the harm a steady diet of such food could cause growing children? I know what these commercial outfits are trying to do. They want to expand their market and profits at the expense of unsuspecting children and their parents."

"Please, Alice, don't exaggerate what may happen here," Mr. Sinn responded. "Besides, the school's PTO has endorsed the concept of this school-business partnership because it sees the value to the school in the long run. After the testing period is over, we still have the computer lab."

Ms. Hammersmith understood the principal's apparent motive for this partnership and had an idea of what a state-of-the-art personal computer lab would cost the school district without the fast food company's assistance. But she could not accept the apparent unconcern for the nutritional health of Craig School's pupils. She was personally affronted because she was not consulted about the idea to begin with, let alone the substance of negotiations with the company.

"Jack," the dietician said, "I'm going to leave this list of fast foods and their caloric and fat content with you to study. And my next stop will be the superintendent's office." Ms. Hammersmith then turned and left Mr. Sinn's office without saying goodbye.

Mr. Sinn, now quite concerned, looked at the list.

6 chicken nuggets	290 calories	51% fat
tuna sandwich (4 oz., oil)	701 calories	62% fat
2 hot dogs (no bun, chicken)	232 calories	70% fat
3-1/2 oz. turkey breast on large croissant	462 calories	41% fat
1 oz. blue tortilla chips	155 calories	52% fat
green salad with 3 tablespoons of Thousand Island dressing	201 calories	76% fat
fish sandwich (breaded, deep fried with tartar sauce)	488 calories	50% fat
3-1/2 oz. beefburger, lettuce, tomato and ketchup	260 calories	33% fat
trail mix (1/2 cup)	316 calories	68% fat

The principal stopped reading the list after the trail mix entry. He turned and gazed out the window. He saw the gleeful pupils running, shouting, jumping as they gathered by the school's main doors ready for the school day to begin. Mr. Sinn thought that such high energy could burn up all those calories on the list, but the fat content of the fast foods on the list did concern him. The principal remembered how the school district's other elementary principals had rejected the overtures of the fast food company on grounds that they opposed the commercialization of their schools and the high public profile their schools would have because of the testing program. He began to have second thoughts about the partnership. He reached for his telephone and started to dial the superintendent's office number.

QUESTIONS FOR DISCUSSION

1. Should Jack Sinn have discussed his plans with the dietician before dealing with the McClarence company? Why? How would Hoy and Miskel's concepts of expertise and relevancy apply here?
2. What decision-making steps should a principal take when dealing with requests for the students to enter outside-of-school contests, for making agreements with businesses, or any community organization?
3. If the purposes of the schools are to balance, purify, and simplify the world for students, how are those purposes useful in helping the principal make a decision in this instance?
4. What contingencies or factors should the principal consider when dealing with vendors who propose to materially help the school? In what ways would a local school council in a site-based management school influence decisions that need to be made here?
5. Should the principal apply the decision rules in taking action in this circumstance? Why or why not?

Ethnic And Racial Problems

HOLDING HANDS IS NOT PART OF THE CURRICULUM

At 2:30 P.M. Mr. Antonio, the principal, sat back in his chair and began to mull over the school's progress in solving the problems caused by the recent desegregation activities of the district. Coombe Elementary School had been all white. The district busing plan had changed the school population to 85 percent white and 15 percent black. He felt that the children were getting along well and there had been no parental unpleasant or aggressive behavior.

To help the integration process, Mr. Antonio had encouraged the teachers to place black and white children together whenever there were classroom groups and projects. He had made a special effort to encourage black parents to attend PTA meetings and encouraged the sponsors of extracurricular activities to get black students to participate.

Next week Mrs. Breen would be staging her school musical. Mr. Antonio had been told that the children were getting along well and working together. He was disturbed by the phone call he had received earlier from Mr. Dillon. Dillon stated that he didn't mind blacks being bussed into the school, but he is vigorously opposed to his daughter dancing with a black boy, hugging him in the musical, and spending so much time with blacks. He also objected to the usual party that Mrs. Breen gives for the cast after the musical. Either Mrs. Breen would change his daughter's partner, or he would not allow her to participate in the musical. Mr. Antonio replied, "The placing of children into particular roles in the musical is Mrs. Breen's responsibility. Not only would your daughter learn a great deal from being in the play, but she also is enjoying playing a lead role." Mr. Dillon replied, "I see I am the first one to call you about my feelings. I expect you will get five more calls from other parents who are going to make the same request. I want to thank you for listening to me. I will call you in three days to find out what you intend to do. Goodbye."

Indeed, that day Mr. Antonio received five more calls with a similar request from parents. Mr. Antonio had written a note to Mrs. Breen to see him that afternoon at 2:45 P.M. He wondered what possible strategies they could develop to solve this problem.

QUESTIONS FOR DISCUSSION

1. What approach do you think Mr. Antonio, the principal, was attempting to use with Mr. Dillon? How effective do you think it was?
2. What specific actions might Mr. Antonio take to provide emotional support and build trust between the parties in this situation? Can he remain neutral? Should he?
3. What rights or values seem to be in conflict in this instance?
4. At what point might a principal want to apprise the central office of a conflict?
5. At what point, if any, might a principal want to request outside help from the central office? What are the pros and cons of doing so?
6. What school and community resources might Mr. Antonio utilize in seeking a resolution?

JOSÉ WANTS TO GO TO THE CIRCUS

Mr. Rubin, the principal of Jeffrey Elementary School, has been informed by Mrs. Auira, the coordinator of the six special education teachers (3 classes of T. M. H., 1 class of E. M. H., and 2 classes for the partially sighted), that all arrangements for the circus trip the next day were complete. The buses will leave the school at 12:30 P.M. and return about 6:30 P.M.

The next morning at 9:00 A.M. Mr. Rubin received a telephone call from Mrs. Rodriquez. She was very upset because her son, José, was excluded from the circus trip. She accused Mrs. Auira of discrimination. Furthermore, all the children in José's class "have problems" and that was no reason to exclude only him. After all, isn't that why the children are in a special program with a small enrollment and specially trained teachers. Unless José goes, Mrs. Rodriquez said she would contact her alderman, the P. T. O. president, the attorney in the storefront office, and someone to see about getting Mrs. Auira fired. "I bet if José had a Puerto Rican teacher, he would be going on the circus trip," Mrs. Rodriquez lamented.

QUESTIONS FOR DISCUSSION

1. Should Mr. Rubin refer the call to Mrs. Auira or attempt to deal with the matter himself? Why?
2. If you would decide to deal with the call yourself, how would you proceed? If not, how would you proceed with delegating it?

3. As Mr. Rubin, what would be your reaction to the threats made by Mrs. Rodriquez? Would your reaction be what you would want it to be? Explain.
4. What additional information might help Mr. Rubin make an accurate assessment of the situation? How could he obtain such information?
5. How can a principal be both responsive to the parent while not betraying trust and confidence in the teacher?

PARENTS OF BUSSED CHILDREN

The racial composition of Hayes Elementary School had been recently changed because of court ordered desegregation. The enrollment of the school is now 75 percent white and 25 percent minority. The building is located in a white suburblike area in a large city. The community is vigorously against the bussing program. They are not opposed to black students being bussed into the school but see no sense in bussing white students into black areas. Enrollment is now 800 students.

The present president of the PTA has a strong commitment to public education and to the PTA's mission. At the beginning of the school year there were no minority group members. Attempts to get the minority parents did not produce acceptable representation. At each meeting some minority parents would attend, but they did not return for the next meeting. A publicity campaign that included students hand carrying announcements of the meeting home and other notices being sent to the local newspaper was employed to increase minority attendance.

The principal and the PTA president were disappointed at the results but managed to get the motion to elect officers tabled. Almost all the PTA members agreed that for the organization to be viable, it needed parent interest and attendance. At the next meeting officers were elected. Although a few minority parents were in attendance, they were unknown by the other parents and none were elected as PTA officers. At the end of the meeting, the principal walked to the office and started to list things to be done that would make the parents of the bussed children feel a part of the school community.

QUESTIONS FOR DISCUSSION

1. What would you include on the principal's list?
2. Is this an intragroup or an intergroup conflict? Why do you think so?

3. Is the principal's desire to get the parents of the minority students involved in the PTA a part of his official responsibility? Is it a proper part of a principal's role? Is it likely to succeed?
4. What, if any, unique or special considerations might apply to work with minority groups? What experience have you had in that regard? What authority could you cite to support your views?
5. What school and community resources might be useful in this situation, and how could they be utilized?
6. Describe the culture of this school in terms of Deal and Kennedy's conclusions about highly successful businesses.

A RACIALLY INTEGRATED SCHOOL?

The principal of Lincoln Elementary School, Judd Soler, walked into his office and saw a large stack of mail he needed to examine. This was his first day as principal. He had previously taught seventh and eighth grade math at a desegregated school that was 50 percent black. This was one reason he got the job. The school population at Lincoln was 30 percent each of whites, blacks, and Hispanics and 10 percent Asians. The school's population was representative of the surrounding community.

As he looked through his mail, Mr. Soler came across several notes from teachers and parents. Mrs. Jones, a fifth grade teacher, wrote the following:

Dear Mr. Soler:

I want to tell you that I will give you my support for improving the educational standards at Lincoln. We have many at-risk children and the educational standards have been dropping for the last five years. May I suggest we have a review of the grading policies at the school.

Mr. Soler then opened a letter from Mrs. Rodrigues.

Dear Mr. Soler:

Welcome. As president of the Hispanic Cultural Club I would like to talk with you about our Hispanic children. They are not making the progress we think they should and we feel there is not enough emphasis placed on Hispanic culture. Furthermore, couldn't we introduce the Spanish language in our curriculum?

Another note was from Mrs. Smith, a parent.

Dear Mr. Soler:

I am so happy you are our principal. Mrs. Brown, a parent from your previous school, said what a wonderful teacher you were and how much math her children learned in your class. I think you need to do something about a very touchy problem. Last year my son complained that he was being physically threatened by some nonwhite students. They told him that if he didn't give them 25 cents a day, they would beat him up. I don't know how widespread this is, but would you please look into this?

He opened another letter.

Dear Principal:

We, the black parents of Lincoln Elementary School, would like to say how much we appreciate your becoming our principal. As you know, there are problems in the curriculum. Teachers have lower expectations (they think our children can't do as well as the whites) for our black children. There is also a general distrust by the parents of other ethnic groups. Please call me at your convenience to discuss this problem.

Sincerely,
Mark Green

As Mr. Soler was going through more of the mail, Mr. Wills, the assistant principal, came in. He said, "I want you to know that we have a difficult problem here. When school closed in June we were having too many discipline problems both in the classroom and in the general areas. In the lunchroom we were having frequent food fights and on the playground there were many rules being broken. I am not sure if they are racial in nature or the result of our lax discipline policy. I think the first thing we need to do is to tighten up our discipline policy. We need to get parent support. Is there anything you want me to do?"

Mr. Soler said, "Thanks, Al, let me do some thinking."

Mr. Soler looked at the letters he had received and mulled over the assistant principal's remarks. He began to feel somewhat disturbed. His neck seemed to tighten up. He thought, "I need to meditate for ten minutes before I start on these problems. I am too tense."

QUESTIONS FOR DISCUSSION

1. What situational factors does Mr. Soler need to consider before he exercises his leadership in the school?
2. How could the principal apply a decision-making model to deal with this situation?
3. After Mr. Soler decides what his problem is should he notify the superintendent to let him know what is going on in the school? What categories of conflict are at work here?
4. What educational values does Mr. Soler need to examine to focus on the problems presented to him? How does Lipham's decision-making model provide for the inclusion of values?
5. If Mr. Soler decides that he needs to consult with the various leaders of each ethnic group, should he consult first with the leaders or with the school community as a whole? What kind of negotiations strategy should he use during the consultations?

Parent Preferences

THE TEACHER ISN'T ANY GOOD

Mrs. Norridge entered the principal's office. Her son, John, was eleven years old and was in Mr. Kroll's sixth grade. John had difficulties in school. He was disruptive, missed assignments, and had difficulty remaining in his seat.

Mrs. Norridge began the conversation, "I want my son transferred from Mr. Kroll's room. Mr. Kroll is too young, too inexperienced. Certainly, he does not know how to reach my son. In addition, he has been lax in notifying me about my son's missing assignments. Why did he wait three weeks before informing me of my son's inadequacies? I want John transferred to a qualified teacher like Mr. Dubin. My daughter was in his class. She did very well with him. The problem stems from personality differences."

QUESTIONS FOR DISCUSSION

1. Can the principal be a neutral party in this situation? Why or why not?
2. What would be an effective strategy for the principal to use?
3. How might this conflict develop into a win/lose situation? What could happen?
4. How might the principal attempt to produce a win/win solution?

5. When should a principal become directly involved in a conflict between a parent and a teacher, and when should the strategy be to stay uninvolved? Or only slightly involved? Which seems to be the case in this instance?

6. First describe what the principal would do using a human relations approach; then a human resources approach.

REWARDING BAD BEHAVIOR?

Tom Horn, a seventh grader, had a hostile and spiteful attitude toward teachers and some students, and he put forth little effort in his school work. He was a difficult child to teach. Mrs. Horn, Tom's mother, thought Tom was a gifted child that the school could not reach.

At the Block Elementary School, there was a tradition that the students perform in a skit on Parents' Night. Tom showed a talent for drama and was assigned a major role in the skit by English teacher, Kitty Fourndear.

Kitty wanted Tom released for a week along with the others in the skit at 2:00 P.M. each day in order to rehearse the skit properly. All the students except Tom were released by their teachers. Ms. Carol Crothers, Tom's social studies teacher, refused to excuse Tom because he was doing poor work and was a discipline problem. She believed that releasing Tom would be rewarding bad behavior. Ms. Fourndear thought that Tom's attitude toward school, his relationships with students, and his sense of personal worth may have improved because of activity in the skit. She believed that everything else had been tried and nothing had modified his behavior.

Tom told his mother that he could not rehearse the skit because of his social studies teacher. Mrs. Horn then contacted and complained to Ms. Fourndear. The next day Tom's mother and Ms. Fourndear went to the principal to ask him to intervene.

QUESTIONS FOR DISCUSSION

1. Which of the obstructionist behaviors might be the most likely for the principal to rely upon? Representativeness? Availability? Adjustment/Anchoring? Why do you think so?

2. Which teacher has the most reasonable position? Defend your answer.

3. Is the principal's role in this situation most properly that of a neutral party or an advocate? Why?

4. Which model of decision making might best fit the situation, and how could it be applied?

5. What parties might be involved in the decision-making process? Why include or exclude certain parties?
6. What might be a larger issue between Ms. Fourndear and Ms. Crothers? If there is, how might the principal approach that issue?
7. Are the views on discipline reflective of a human resources approach or a human relations approach?

A PARENT'S AND A TEACHER'S REQUEST

Mrs. Wicklow left a note for the principal, Mr. Oakley. "Mr. Oakley: I want to be sure that Jack does not get Ms. Styles for sixth grade. Two years ago Simon had a terrible time with her. Both my husband and I are rather adamant about this. Ms. Styles is too much of a disciplinarian, and I don't want a hysterical and unhappy child for another year. Sincerely, Mrs. Eva Wicklow."

Mr. Oakley needed to refresh his memory and looked at the assignment of children to the sixth grade teachers. The fifth grade teachers had been asked if there should be any changes in the class organization. Both had responded similarly in that they felt each group was cohesive and achieving, though there were discipline problems, and should continue to be heterogeneously organized.

That afternoon, Mr. Oakley met separately with the two sixth grade teachers, Mr. Chart and Ms. Styles. Mr. Chart thought it would be best to maintain the classes as organized. He didn't think it was the parents' prerogative to assign their children to a class. That was the school's responsibility, particularly the principal. In addition, he didn't think it would be good for Jack to be singled out and placed into a strange class. Later that afternoon, Mr. Oakley met with Ms. Styles. Ms. Styles felt it would be a superior idea to change Jack. She had a terrible year with Simon and his parents. Simon had average ability and was somewhat shy. Both of Simon's parents were on her back the whole year.

"They were under the illusion that Simon had superior intelligence and that the reason Simon did not get A's in all his subjects was because the other teachers or myself were at fault. I would appreciate it if you changed Jack. You would be doing me a favor and satisfying the parents."

Mr. Oakley started to wonder what he should do.

QUESTIONS FOR DISCUSSION

1. What evaluation would you make of Mr. Oakley's strategy up to this point?

2. Based on the information at hand, would you guess that Mr. Oakley is an authoritarian/autocratic decision maker or a participatory decision maker? Why do you think so?

3. Where would you place Mr. Oakley on the "Authority-Freedom Continuum" developed by Tannenbaum and Schmidt (Figure 2.1)? Is that placement the optimal point on the continuum, or would a different point be more appropriate in your opinion? Why?

4. Is there a way for both teachers to save face while arriving at an educationally sound decision? What might that be? How could it be changed?

5. Would a Quality Circle (QC) be appropriate as a means of making class assignments? As the principal, would you suggest such an approach?

SEPARATED PARENTS

Mr. Edwards, Bob's father, walked into the office at 11:15 A.M. and requested to see Mrs. Chapel, the principal of Wrightwood Elementary School. Bob Edwards was a bright fifth grader, but in the last year, he had become a discipline problem. He began to have behavioral difficulties since divorce proceedings began between his parents. The conferences Mrs. Chapel and Bob's teacher had with Bob's mother were not helpful. Her hatred for Mr. Edwards seemed to blind her thinking about Bob. She constantly slandered Mr. Edwards' character and behavior. She had sent a note to Mrs. Chapel stating they were separated, and under no circumstances was Mr. Edwards to see Bob in, or take him from, the school.

Mrs. Chapel came to the office counter to talk with Mr. Edwards. He said, "I have made an appointment with the psychologist for noon today, and I want to take Bob with me now. You know he needs some help."

QUESTIONS FOR DISCUSSION

1. How could Mrs. Chapel determine the school's proper response to Mr. Edwards' request?

2. What potential problems could develop from this situation? List as many as there appear to be within the realm of possibility.

3. As Mrs. Chapel, under what conditions might you consent to send Bob with his father?
4. Under what conditions would you believe you could not consent to Mr. Edwards' request?
5. What school district policies and state laws would apply in your school district? If you do not know, how can you find out?
6. How could a human resources approach apply to a student like Bob Edwards?

A DISINTERESTED PARENT?

Marvin Johnson, who is in the third grade, has been a sullen child. Recently, he was found sitting on a bench outside the principal's office. On the referral card sent to Mr. Beck, the principal, Ms. Clancey, the teacher, stated that Marvin started a fight in the classroom.

Since he scored very low on a reading test last May, Marvin's teacher, counselor, and the principal have agreed that another year in third grade would provide Marvin some time to "catch up." His mother has not attended any conferences about Marvin's progress at the school. However, over the telephone she has said to Ms. Clancey, "Do what you think is best."

Marvin never smiled or laughed. He rarely did homework and was absent approximately once every seven days. What school work he did do was inaccurate and sloppy, and a time-on-task analysis showed him to be on task only 30 percent of the time. His sister, who is in the first grade, has made good progress since she started grade school two months ago.

After school each day, Marvin and his sister go home and are unsupervised until their mother comes home from work. When asked what he does after school for the three hours until his mother comes home, Marvin stated that he and his sister watch television.

Ms. Clancey, his present teacher, tried to have conferences with Marvin's mother, but Mrs. Johnson replied that she was a single parent, and she could not take off work. She had plenty to do just with her six-year old child and had said the school should do what they think best for Marvin.

Ms. Clancey complained to Mr. Beck that Marvin has done less and less classwork. He has disrupted his classmates and become more physically aggressive. He has pushed children in line and initiated fights on the playground. He has become a classic bully.

Mr. Beck began to think about the situation and what he could do to "turn Marvin around."

QUESTIONS FOR DISCUSSION

1. What practical positive steps could Mr. Beck provide Ms. Clancey for dealing with Marvin? Could the application of a human resources approach to this problem work here? Why or why not?

2. How does a school principal deal with a single parent who appears to be operating under continuous crisis and/or who appears to be disinterested?

3. What are some community agencies that may be helpful to Marvin's mother?

4. What criteria should be used for retention? How could a decision-making model be used to establish criteria?

5. What role should the school take concerning latchkey children? Could the application of the Quality Circle concept be tried here? Why or why not?

Beliefs And Values

I WISH I KNEW THE CONSTITUTION

Mr. Petau, principal of Antilia Elementary School, looked at his appointment book and saw that he was to meet with Mrs. Levine at 1:30 P.M. and with Mr. Zorca at 2:15 P.M. At 1:30 P.M., a distraught and irate Mrs. Levine proceeded to complain that her child's third grade teacher had shown "wanton disregard" of her son's Jewish heritage by presenting a program of Christmas customs to her class. Moreover, she charged that no opportunity was provided for consideration of any other religious orientations. Mrs. Levine demanded an immediate apology from the teacher together with some assurance from the principal that there would be no repetition of this type of activity.

At 2:15 P.M., a tense but calm Mr. Zorca entered Mr. Petau's office. Mr. Zorca said, "I am outraged by the religious brainwashing that is going on in this school. It is obscene. There is a constitutional separation of church and state. I am opposed to the Christmas carols sung in the halls by the Glee Club. My son was subjected to a play about the Christ myth. You know! The one in the manger. And worst of all is the kind of blackmail that teachers use to get Christmas presents from the kids. This kind of behavior must cease!"

QUESTIONS FOR DISCUSSION

1. Are you aware of similar objections in your own or surrounding districts? What were the specific issues in those instances? How were the objections handled by appropriate persons?
2. What is your understanding of the intent of the U.S. Constitution and its subsequent interpretation by the U.S. Supreme Court of the proper role of religion in public education?
3. Do the instances described by the two parents seem to you to present a questionable introduction of religion into the public school? Why or why not?
4. Aside from your personal views, how would you attempt to respond to the parents?
5. What school policy might guide you? If your school had no policy on this subject, would you think it might be wise to develop one? If so, how would you do so, and who should be involved?
6. When it comes to religion, are there permissible shared values that could be fostered in the public school? Why or why not?

AN EYE FOR AN EYE

Michael Karn, a fourth grade pupil, established his power among his classmates by threats that were not mere verbalizations. He had claimed ownership of money, sweaters, and school supplies which he had taken away from his classmates. Initial protests by his classmates became silent when the teacher began to investigate the complaints to determine ownership. Michael always was the owner.

The teacher asked the children to bring a hard cover, loose-leaf notebook to school and told them to put their name, address, and room number on the inside cover. The following day, Michael did not bring a notebook to class. By three o'clock of the same day, the teacher broke up a fight between Al and Michael. The fight was about the ownership of a notebook. Al had apparently decided not to give in to Michael. An examination of the notebook showed that Michael's name appeared over a name which had been erased. Michael also stated that his mother told him that it was his notebook.

The teacher called Michael's mother and asked her to come to school with Michael at 8:30 the following morning. Michael reported to the teacher the following day that his mother would come later in the morning. At 10:30 A.M., Michael's mother walked into the room while the teacher was conducting a lesson and demanded, "Now what's this notebook business about? . . . I told Michael to take the notebook; kids are always taking his things, and I've told him that if it is okay if they take from him, he can take from them. I see nothing wrong in this. It's not stealing."

The teacher dismissed the children for recess and said to Mrs. Karn, "I think we need to discuss the problem with the principal."

QUESTIONS FOR DISCUSSION

1. As the principal would you perceive Michael's alleged thievery to be a legitimate problem for the teacher to bring to you? Why or why not?
2. If Mrs. Karn persisted in her aggressive attitude, what would you be feeling inside if you were the principal? How would you manage or express those feelings if they were troublesome? Describe the intrapersonal conflict you would be experiencing.
3. What possible negotiations strategies are suggested for the principal by Johnson and Johnson (Table 1.2)?
4. What suggestions would you offer to the mother and the teacher?
5. What suggestions would you offer to the teacher after the mother left your office?
6. What can you do when the values in the homes of some children are in disharmony with the culture of the school?

IS FAITH AN ANSWER?

The end of the school term was approaching and parent-teacher conferences were being scheduled to discuss recommendations for next year's placements. Mrs. John, an early-childhood special education teacher, had frequent contact with Harold Shaw's parents in regard to his academic/social performance and progress during the school year. Harold had had cataract surgery on both eyes, an astigmatism of his left eye, and partial blindness in his right eye. Harold's parents perceived him as having "above normal" intelligence and behavior in all areas, except that of sight. After seven months in a special education program, the teacher, psychologist, social worker, nurse, and vision specialist strongly agreed that continued special education placement be recommended due to Harold's one and one-half year lag in cognitive receptive language, fine and gross motor skills, and social behavior.

After the establishment of a mutually agreeable conference date for the Individual Educational Program (IEP) Team, Mrs. Shaw called the school. She informed the secretary that there was no need for a conference because she and her husband were sure of Harold's ability for success in first grade. Furthermore, the Shaw's faith in God would allow Harold to develop normally from now on.

The principal, upset after returning from another of the district's accountability meetings, was informed of Mrs. Shaw's comments. The principal wondered what her legal, educational, and ethical responsibilities were for Harold's welfare. Moreover, she wondered how she could reason with the parents when their faith had apparently blinded them to any rational discussion of their son's situation. Perhaps, the principal thought, a clergyman might be helpful in getting through to the Shaws on this matter.

QUESTIONS FOR DISCUSSION

1. What are the school's legal, educational, and ethical responsibilities for Harold's welfare?
2. How do these responsibilities shape or influence the school's strategy with the parents, if at all?
3. Who should have primary responsibility for the case, the principal or the special education teacher? Why? Define a role for each.
4. What would you suggest as a strategy with the parents in this instance?
5. If the parents persisted in their view after your best efforts, what would you do? Would the intervention of a clergyman be helpful?
6. How far ought a school go in efforts to ensure the educational opportunity of a child? To what extremes? How much cost? Where do the rights of the parents to practice their religious beliefs end and the rights of the child to adequate education begin? Who decides and how?
7. Do you think the parents feel a vital part of the IEP team? Why? Why not?
8. Could the Quality Circle process provide some insights into effective use of the IEP team?

THE SHORT CUT

Mrs. Salmon came into the principal's office. Before Principal Edgar could say anything, Mrs. Salmon said, "I have been living across the street from the school at 4720 N. Carot for the last twenty years and never had trouble with the children. The last two weeks have been hell. First, these kids are constantly ringing my doorbell and running away. Second, they seem to leave all sorts of junk on my property. I find candy wrappers, notices sent by the school that are supposed to go home to their parents, and torn pieces of bread. Why are they using my property for a garbage can? Third, they are running through my backyard and using it as a short cut. If that is not bad enough, they picked all my crocuses. They are ruining my garden.

"What kind of value system do these kids and their parents have anyway? I sent three of my own children through this school and never had any trouble with the previous principals. Mr. Edgar, what are you going to do about this?"

QUESTIONS FOR DISCUSSION

1. Suggest an opening line for Mr. Edgar.
2. Would your primary interest be in appeasing Mrs. Salmon or in finding a solution to the problem, assuming the problem is as she had stated it? Is appeasement ever a valid option? Why or why not?
3. Considering the different types of conflict, how would this problem be defined?
4. Would you react differently if Mrs. Salmon was a quiet, uninvolved member of the community? An influential member of the power structure of the community? A member of the school board?
5. If you would react differently to any of the above, what strategy would you utilize in each instance? If you would not react differently, why not?

Site-Based Management

AUTHORITARIAN OR LEADER?

Ms. Wyles had been principal of the Johnson Elementary School for the last eleven years. The last year the district had moved to site-based management. A nine member local school council composed of three parents with children in the school, three adults in the community, and three teachers had been elected to the local school council which was empowered to hire and fire the principal, make curricular and programmatic decisions, choose the manner in which Chapter I monies are to be used, and make decisions concerning class size and the assignment of teacher aides. Furthermore, all expenditures needed to be approved by the council and countersigned by the president of the council. The selection of Ms. Wyles had not been perfunctory. Three parent members of the council had not voted for her. They said she was too authoritarian in her demeanor and did not really consider the parent's wishes.

Ms. Wyles believed she knew what was best for the children's education. Though courteous and respectful toward parents, she believed they had no real knowledge about education theory, psychology, administration, supervision, and curriculum. She thought through her decisions, and, at times, asked the faculty for input, but always made decisions based upon educational needs. She felt that if you do a good job educating the students, good community relations will follow.

Johnson Elementary School was located in a transient neighborhood. Around April, the weather got better and gang activity in and around the school began to increase. Not only did adult strangers come into the building, but some of the bolder gang members also entered the school looking for some students to settle a score. Principal Wyles decided to assign the physically strongest aide to help supervise the entrance and the halls. This aide happened to be assigned to the attendance office whose staff was funded with discretionary funds by the local school council. The office had done a good job and indeed had improved student attendance. However, Ms. Wyles thought that security at this time of the year was more important than attendance and decided to transfer the aide without the council's approval. This was not the first time that Ms. Wyles had acted unilaterally in what she considered the best interests of the children.

Ms. Wyles had spent money in October of the school year for textbooks for a special social studies program without waiting for council approval. Some teachers on the faculty had attended a workshop during the summer and wanted to introduce a new social studies program. The principal listened to them and was convinced it would be good for the students and the teachers. The four teachers involved in the program said they could not teach the program without new texts. Many of the old texts were missing and those that were around were falling apart and had missing pages. Because it was October, further delays in getting the textbooks could not help the teachers do justice to the program. There was not enough money in the regular textbook fund so Ms. Wyles decided she would pay for the texts from the discretionary fund. Since the bill would not arrive until after the council had decided to spend these discretionary funds, she approved the purchase and ordered the texts. She told the teachers to carefully develop a proposal for the council to justify the new texts.

Six weeks later the council met. Teachers had been requested to make proposals and enough proposals were presented to spend four times the available discretionary funds. The meeting lasted several hours. The presentation by the teachers of the special social studies program was excellent, and, with the support that Ms. Wyles gave the program, the teachers convinced the council to unanimously support it.

It was later discovered by the council that the principal had ordered the books without its approval. She was told by the council president not to do this again even if it was for what she thought a sound reason.

Shortly after the assignment of the aide, members of the council were visiting the school and noticed the attendance office aide patrolling the halls. They asked the principal why Mark was in the halls and not in the office. The principal replied, "At this time of the year the security of the children is endangered and it seems reasonable to shift the aide from attendance to security during these last few months."

The council members next stopped by the attendance office and asked the secretary why Mark was in the halls. The secretary responded, "Ms. Wyles said she needed Mark for security purposes and told me he would no longer report to the Attendance Office. I told her that Mark is indispensable if we are to keep our enrollment at or above the 90 percent level. Couldn't you find someone else?"

Four weeks later at the next local school council meeting the issue of the staffing of the attendance office was brought up by Mrs. Flint, a parent member. With anger in her voice she said, "This is another example of the authoritarian approach of Ms. Wyles, of her view that the council can be disregarded whenever she wishes, and that she thinks of us merely as rubber stamps. We need to remove her from this school."

The room became very quiet. The president of the council asked for further discussion.

QUESTIONS FOR DISCUSSION

1. What category of conflict is at work here? Explain your choice.
2. How do you think parents evaluate the effectiveness of an elementary school principal? Could they be "staff-developed" to evaluate rationally as council members? Why or why not?
3. How should the principal deal with parents who are antagonistic to his/her style of leadership? What conflict-handling style would be most suitable in such a situation? Explain.
4. Why do you suppose Ms. Wyles did not wait until the next council meeting to get permission to transfer the school aide? Do you think she applied a decision-making model to her action? Why or why not?
5. As principal, how would you respond to Mrs. Flint? Would you apply a negotiations strategy? If so, which one?

REFERENCES

Roland S. Barth, Improving Schools from Within: Teachers, Parents, and Principals Can Make the Difference (San Francisco: Jossey-Bass Inc., Publishers, 1990).

Robert L. Crowson and Cynthia Porter-Gehrie, "The Discretionary Behavior of Principals in Large-City Schools," **Educational Administration Quarterly,** Volume 16, No. 1 (Winter, 1980): 45–69.

Laurence Iannaconne and Frank W. Lutz, **Politics, Power and Policy: The Governing of School Districts** (Columbus, Ohio: Charles E. Merrill Publishers, 1970).

Ralph B. Kimbrough and Michael Y. Nunnery, **Educational Administration: An Introduction,** 3rd ed. (New York: Macmillan Publishing Company, 1988).

Leslie W. Kindred, Don Bagin, and Donald R. Gallagher, **The School and Community Relations,** 4th ed. (Englewood Cliffs, N.J.: Prentice-Hall, 1989).

A New Look at Empowerment: How Educators and Communities can Empower each Other (Arlington, VA: American Association of School Administrators, 1990).

P. E. Peterson, **School Politics Chicago Style** (Chicago: The University of Chicago Press, 1976).

S. B. Sarason, **The Culture of the School and the Problem of Change,** 2nd ed. (Boston: Allyn and Bacon, Inc., 1982).

Susan M. Swat, **Enhancing Parent Involvement in Schools** (New York: Columbia Teachers College Press, 1984).

David E. Wiles, Jon Wiles, and Joseph Bondi, **Practical Politics for School Administrators** (Boston: Allyn and Bacon, Inc., 1981).

District-Wide
Relationships: The Cases

A case study is usually developed out of a real situation. The cases in this chapter provide reality based data whereby case method analysis performed by elementary administration students can assist them to integrate theory and practice.

Presently in the areas of elementary school administration and supervision, there are no current and complete case books. The last case book in elementary school administration was titled **Cases in Elementary School Administration** written by Oscar T. Jarvis, published in 1971. It is now out of print. The most popular case text in school administration is titled **School Leadership and Administration** by Richard Gorton, and the third edition was published in 1987. However, the cases deal primarily with general administrative and secondary school problems rather than special situations that focus on the elementary school. Therefore, the authors have included a set of seven fully developed case studies aimed at the elementary principal's relationships with district-wide issues and problems.

School administration cannot be considered solely as technical management (e.g., developing a budget, assigning teachers, closing a school at the end of the year, etc.). The school administrator also must take into account, for example, community traditions (often ambiguous), student health and safety in transfer cases, and the affective responses from parents and students when school bus routes are changed. Examination of these latter tasks indicates that interpersonal skills are necessary for their successful completion. District office administrators and supervisors rely on the support of the principals to help them fulfill their own organizational roles. Therefore, building or "field" administrators are sometimes asked and sometimes compelled to participate in district-wide decision making that calls for both technical management and interpersonal skills.

Principal relations with the district office usually occur through the district superintendent. For specific purposes, especially in larger school districts, principals may communicate periodically with other district level administrators (e.g., assistant superintendent, business manager, director of special education, etc.). Principals are quick to discover the temperament of district office personnel and sense the indifference or concern for the principal's organizational role and problems. District office personnel who emphasize efficiency (time, schedules, finances, etc.) at the expense of human welfare or equity can be detrimental to principals' morale.

The superintendent establishes the climate of relations with the principals. If the superintendent enjoys the responsibility, possesses concern for others, works cooperatively with other personnel, and has an "open door" communications policy, successful district-wide administration is possible.

The elementary school principal is in close proximity with instructional and noninstructional staff. Therefore, the principal communicates and translates the philosophy and policies of the district office. Hence, district office personnel in general, the superintendent in particular, and building principals are interrelated and interdependent. When the interrelationships break down or are rejected by either party, both the district office and the schools suffer the negative consequences. The case studies in this chapter involve problems in the network of relationships and interdependencies between elementary principals, the district office, and/or the school board.

In a changing society, many administrative decisions and policies are made in an atmosphere of social tension and conflict. Thus a close working relationship between building principals and district office personnel requires continuous communications based on a participative style of leadership. If the superintendent and other district level staff are going to resolve current problems and plan for the district's future, the elementary principal's organizational role and professional outlook must be supportive of these district-wide efforts. How that role can be appropriately and successfully supportive will be a concern of students who seek to resolve the potential and apparent conflicts in the case studies of this chapter.

CASE STUDY NUMBER 1

CLOSING A SCHOOL: LOYALTY OR EFFICIENCY

At the last meeting of the Valley View Elementary School District Board of Education, a report was presented by the superintendent on the financial condition of the District along with some general projections about the budgets for the next and succeeding school years. This report indicated that the revenue for this year was somewhat more than had been predicted and would be reflected by a projected increase in the year-end balance from $13,900 to $182,000.

The projected budget for the next school year indicates that revenues and expenditures will be approximately equal. The projection is based on several assumptions which were clearly stated in the report.

However, when the same assumptions excluding any salary increases are used to project the revenues and expenditures for the succeeding school year, the budget will show that expenditures will exceed revenues by approximately $500,000. If salaries are included at the rate of $50,000 for each 1 percent increase, the excess of expenditures over revenues increases proportionally.

After some discussion of these projections, the Board directed the elementary principals to consider options, in consultation with the superintendent, whereby the projected deficit for the succeeding school year could be reduced.

The Board's "shopping list" of options for reducing the budget was presented to the principals.

The list included the following which could be accomplished in the next school year:

1. *Reduction in staff due to drop in enrollment.*
   Board predictions indicate that elementary school enrollment will drop approximately fifty students for the next year. With this loss of students and the increased use of multiage groupings, the staff could show some decrease.

2. *Reduction or elimination of educational programs.*
   Such programs could include the following:
   a. Transitional First Grade
   b. Music Program
   c. Physical Education Program
   d. Extracurricular Activities
   e. Library Program
   f. Preschool Screening

All these programs were considered for similar action when severe budget reductions were made several years ago. With the exception of the Library Program and Transitional First Grade, the programs were either completely eliminated or drastically reduced. Since that time, all have been partially or completely restored but at reduced spending levels.

3. *Implementation of an Early Retirement Plan.*

   The Board is presently preparing an Early Retirement Incentive Plan. Hopefully, a plan will be adopted which will be available for consideration by the staff before the end of the present school year.

4. *Continued monitoring of energy use.*

   Energy expense continues to be a greater and greater drain on finances. Some funds may be available from outside sources to assist in correcting some of the conditions which cause large amounts of energy use. Unfortunately, the Board does not have the expertise to determine which corrective measures will be cost effective. As a consequence, the Board desires an energy audit by trained personnel to provide the District with information which can be used to direct future efforts in this area.

In addition to items listed above, the Board must also consider other items if the budget is to be reduced by an amount which will allow the District to operate in a fiscally responsible manner.

The amount of money available to the District is directly related to the Average Daily Attendance (ADA). As the ADA decreases in a facility, the per student cost increases. However, rarely does such an increase in per student cost improve the educational benefit for individual students enrolled in a regular program. Consequently, individual facility costs are causing the educational program for the District to suffer. The continued operation of some facilities must be questioned. To answer this dilemma, the Board has given some thought to the consolidation of facilities in order to provide a maximum number of dollars for the educational program of all students.

A decision to close buildings would be considered only after a study of enrollment projections. The Board estimates a reduction of some 250 pupils within five years. In addition, the Board has determined the student capacity of each facility assuming that the present programs and organizational structure will continue. Those capacities are as follows:

Building	Present	Capacity
North View	341	425
South View	427	500
Leland Heights	511	675
Valley Knoll	469	500
Pleasant Lane	227	275
John Adams	152	350
Thomas Jefferson	316	400
Washington Irving	556	550

When the present enrollments and the capacity of the facilities are considered, it may be possible to suggest that some facilities be consolidated and at the same time effect some reorganization of the District grade structure.

The Board asked the elementary principals to present their positions on the Board's "shopping list" of concerns and budget reductions at the next regular meeting of the Board in one month. The principals are to make a preliminary presentation first to the superintendent and then, through him, their final recommendations to the Board.

The elementary principals were stunned. They found it difficult to know where to begin. Should they seek the guidance of the superintendent? Should they poll their faculties, parents, neighborhood communities? Do they need a crash course on budgeting? Their university programs never trained them for this contingency. They immediately realized, however, that the recommendations they would make could alter the quality as well as quantity of education in their respective schools for many years to come. The educational future of the community's elementary school children would ride on the recommendations of the elementary principals. Somberly, but with determination, they turned to this crucial task.

The District and each facility's expenditures budgets follow.

DISTRICT BUDGET

	Last Year	Current Year	Next Year
Administration	371,025	382,673	393,449
Instruction	3,172,064	3,170,361	3,678,169
Pupil Personnel Services	135,641	157,625	171,242
Health Services	66,417	68,049	78,697
Pupil Transportation Services	339,793	369,721	438,568
Operation & Maintenance of Plant	915,921	956,145	1,118,169
Fixed Charges	556,945	667,553	703,881
Food Services	7,921	12,385	7,921
Student Activities	75,441	90,177	107,113
Community Services	11,768	13,176	18,321
Capital Outlay	238,267	18,271	91,150
Debt Service	997,357	1,044,370	998,371
Interrupted Payments	217,185	244,208	270,946
Budgetary Reserve	-0-	-0-	50,000
Totals	7,105,745	7,194,714	8,125,997

NORTH VIEW

	Last Year	Current Year	Next Year
Administration	28,909	30,183	31,362
Instruction	346,054	346,758	402,300
Pupil Personnel Services	14,836	17,240	18,730
Health Services	7,264	7,443	8,607
Pupil Transportation Services	37,165	40,438	47,968
Operation and Maintenance of Plant	100,179	104,578	122,300
Fixed Charges	60,916	73,014	76,987
Food Services	866	1,355	866
Student Activities	8,251	9,863	11,715
Community Services	1,287	1,441	2,004
Totals	605,727	632,313	722,839

SOUTH VIEW

	Last Year	Current Year	Next Year
Administration	39,753	34,209	35,556
Instruction	396,633	396,295	459,771
Pupil Personnel Services	16,955	19,703	21,405
Health Services	8,302	8,506	9,837
Pupil Transportation Services	42,474	46,215	54,821
Operation and Maintenance of Plant	114,490	119,518	139,771
Fixed Charges	69,618	83,444	87,985
Food Services	990	1,548	990
Student Activities	9,430	11,272	13,389
Community Services	1,471	1,647	2,290
Totals	700,116	722,357	825,815

LELAND HEIGHTS

	Last Year	Current Year	Next Year
Administration	40,441	42,261	43,945
Instruction	495,791	495,369	574,714
Pupil Personnel Services	21,194	24,629	26,756
Health Services	10,378	10,633	12,296
Pupil Transportation Services	53,093	57,769	68,526
Operation and Maintenance of Plant	143,113	149,398	174,714
Fixed Charges	87,023	104,305	109,981
Food Services	1,238	1,935	1,238
Student Activities	11,788	14,090	16,736
Community Services	1,839	2,059	2,863
Totals	865,898	902,448	1,031,769

VALLEY KNOLL

	Last Year	Current Year	Next Year
Administration	36,597	38,235	39,751
Instruction	446,212	445,832	517,242
Pupil Personnel Services	19,074	22,166	24,081
Health Services	9,340	9,569	11,067
Pupil Transportation Services	47,783	51,992	61,674
Operation and Maintenance of Plant	128,801	134,458	157,242
Fixed Charges	78,320	93,875	98,983
Food Services	1,114	1,742	1,114
Student Activities	10,609	12,681	15,063
Community Services	1,655	1,853	2,576
Totals	779,505	812,403	928,793

PLEASANT LANE

	Last Year	Current Year	Next Year
Administration	25,065	26,157	27,167
Instruction	297,475	297,221	344,828
Pupil Personnel Services	12,716	14,777	16,054
Health Services	6,227	6,380	7,378
Pupil Transportation Services	31,856	34,661	41,116
Operation and Maintenance of Plant	85,868	89,639	104,828
Fixed Charges	52,214	62,583	65,989
Food Services	743	1,161	743
Student Activities	7,073	8,454	10,042
Community Services	1,103	1,235	1,718
Totals	520,340	542,268	619,863

JOHN ADAMS

	Last Year	Current Year	Next Year
Administration	22,643	23,644	24,574
Instruction	272,685	272,453	316,093
Pupil Personnel Services	11,657	13,546	14,716
Health Services	5,708	5,848	6,763
Pupil Transportation Services	29,201	31,773	37,689
Operation and Maintenance of Plant	78,712	82,169	96,093
Fixed Charges	47,862	57,368	60,490
Food Services	681	1,064	681
Student Activities	6,483	7,750	9,205
Community Services	1,011	1,132	1,574
Totals	476,643	496,747	567,878

THOMAS JEFFERSON

	Last Year	Current Year	Next Year
Administration	26,987	28,170	29,264
Instruction	322,264	321,990	373,564
Pupil Personnel Services	13,776	16,009	17,392
Health Services	6,745	6,911	7,993
Pupil Transportation Services	34,510	37,550	44,542
Operation and Maintenance of Plant	93,023	97,108	113,564
Fixed Charges	56,565	67,798	71,488
Food Services	804	1,258	804
Student Activities	7,662	9,159	10,879
Community Services	1,195	1,338	1,861
Totals	563,531	587,291	671,351

WASHINGTON IRVING

	Last Year	Current Year	Next Year
Administration	47,130	49,314	51,334
Instruction	594,950	594,443	689,657
Pupil Personnel Services	25,433	29,555	32,108
Health Services	12,453	12,759	14,756
Pupil Transportation Services	63,711	69,323	82,232
Operation and Maintenance of Plant	171,735	179,277	209,657
Fixed Charges	104,427	125,166	131,978
Food Services	1,485	2,322	1,485
Student Activities	14,145	16,908	20,084
Community Services	2,207	2,471	3,435
Totals	1,037,676	1,081,538	1,236,726

QUESTIONS FOR DISCUSSION

1. What is your evaluation of the Board's "shopping list"? What items would you support for reductions? Which would you oppose? What would be your arguments in each case?
2. The case study reports little about district educational goals. How would your evaluation of the "shopping list" be related to goals for a school district? Do you need or want a "guiding vision"?
3. What is your response to the option of closing buildings? What are the pros and cons of building closings? What factors ought to be considered in deciding which buildings to close? In what ways is the information on building enrollments and capacities helpful? Not helpful?
4. As you review the district budget, what conclusions do you draw? What questions emerge?
5. As you review the individual building level budgets, and compare them, what conclusions do you draw? What questions emerge?
6. Having reviewed the information provided, what other options could you suggest for cost reduction?
7. What constituencies would you involve or consult in your task as a principal? Why? How? Would you apply the Quality Circles concept?

8. Is what the School Board asked the principals to do a good example of the application of the human resources approach to the management of people? Why or why not?

Simulation exercise: The case material lends itself to a simulation format. For example, members of the class may each be assigned a role: superintendent, principals, assistant principals, board members, etc. The goal is to develop recommendations for the superintendent to make to the board.

CASE STUDY NUMBER 2

AN UNACCEPTABLE REPORT CARD

Ms. Cleery, secretary to Mr. Fred Blank, principal of East Borosville Elementary School, has just finished underlining the article on page 1 of the **Morning Sun** when the principal came in.

"Good morning, Mr. Blank. Here is the morning paper. You'd better read it."

"Good morning, Ms. Cleery. I haven't time to read the paper now. I've got to work fast today to quiet the storm over the new elementary report cards."

"Well, you'd better read this article anyway, before you start your work."

Fred Blank, who also was chairman of the pupil evaluation committee, scanned the front page until his eyes were drawn to the underscored article.

> LOCAL GROUP CHIDES NEW SCHOOL REPORT SYSTEM
> October 15. The Citizens League for Elementary Education Now (CLEEN) last night voted overwhelmingly to demand a return to the old report cards in the elementary schools. There was general agreement with the point of view expressed by at least three speakers who claimed the "P" (pass) and "F" (fail) gave little or no information and that pass could mean anything from A plus to D minus. Furthermore, it was important to apply standards at an early age, and parents were entitled to know the progress of their children.

Borosville was an upper middle-class suburban community within commuting distance of a large industrial city. It was the home of a considerable number of business and professional people, and these citizens were most concerned about standards in the elementary school. With few exceptions, the parents in this group were looking ahead to college and tended to have high aspirations for their children.

Fred Blank reread the article. Ms. Cleery's voice interrupted his thought.

"Mrs. Carter from the Citizens League is on the phone. Will you speak with her?"

Fred hesitated a moment. He was surprised, hurt, and angry, and he wasn't really prepared to talk with anyone on this matter, let alone a member of the Citizens League. He barely knew Mrs. Carter. For an instant he was tempted to have his secretary announce that he was busy. Then, with a shrug, he told Ms. Cleery to connect his phone.

"Hello, Mr. Blank? I'm Mrs. Carter from the Citizens League. You've seen the morning papers no doubt. I'm sorry that we felt that we had to take things into our own hands. I assure you that there was nothing personal in this. We simply felt that nothing would be done about our complaints unless we got together and took action."

"Well, I'm glad you called, Mrs. Carter, but I wish that we could have talked this out first and—"

"But we've felt that phone calls to you and the other principals have done little good. It is very hard for parents to get themselves heard. I'm sure that you and some of your teachers had good reasons for the new change, but we as parents have rights and feel that we are entitled to know exactly how our children are doing. And there is one more thing, Mr. Blank. There are many teachers who think the way we do. They did not feel like speaking up at the meeting, but we have heard from them. The Citizens League has delegated me to contact you to find out what you are going to do about our resolution."

"Mrs. Carter, you will have to give me a little time to respond to your resolution. I am not prepared to deal with it at the moment." After that comment Mr. Blank politely, but firmly, said goodbye and hung up the telephone.

Mr. Blank reached for his coffee cup and drank automatically. How had he gotten himself into this dilemma? He thought back over the events that had led to the changing of the pupil report system. He remembered clearly the time, two years before, when the elementary teachers themselves had suggested a new reporting system. He recalled vividly the meeting that he had convened in his school to discuss the widespread expressions of dissatisfaction with the competitive A, B, C, D, E systems. Furthermore, it was the opinion of most of the teachers that the old system was much less objective than it appeared to be. He recalled the superintendent's decision to form a committee to study the best reporting systems of other schools and select him chairman. The committee had brought back a recommendation incorporating the best features of report cards. The new card used "P" and "F" symbols and covered many aspects of the children's development. It clearly stated that at least two conferences per year would be held with parents to discuss in detail the progress of each child. He remembered how the new card had been discussed and then unanimously accepted by the elementary teachers in his school and two of the three other schools. The memories of the past two weeks were the painful ones. When the first report cards had gone home with the letter of explanation, the complaints from parents had kept the phone busy all day. He had heard a rumor that someone was circulating a petition and that it had been signed by prominent citizens. He recalled his efforts to talk to the other elementary principals and his plans to contact parents which he had never had time to put into practice.

The ringing of the telephone interrupted his thinking.

"Mr. Blank, the superintendent is on the line." Fred Blank nodded knowingly.

"Fred, is that you? Can you drop everything and come right over? I'm sure you know what for. We've got to work fast now."

Mr. Blank later returned to his office and faced the dual tasks of reconvening the pupil evaluation committee and arranging for a public meeting for community input into the report system.

QUESTIONS FOR DISCUSSION

1. In hindsight, what steps might Mr. Blank and his committee have taken to gain more advance input into their decision and more support for the final product? What decision-making steps were ignored?

2. What further negative fallout might occur now? Do you support both actions Mr. Blank is now considering? Why or why not?

3. What further suggestions could he make to the superintendent?

4. From your experience, what actions have produced more reaction than was initially expected? What specific issues for local schools are of the type which often elicit strong feelings from various individuals and groups?

5. In complex, loosely-coupled organizations, what strategies are often effective in relating to various interest groups while maintaining organizational integrity?

6. Would you expect Mr. Blank to receive an understanding, helpful response from the superintendent or a critical, blaming response? Why?

7. If you were Mr. Blank, would you attempt to save the new report card system or reverse your position and yield to the vocal critics? Or would you seek some form of compromise? Why?

CASE STUDY NUMBER 3

A FREE AND APPROPRIATE PLACEMENT FOR A PRESCHOOL CHILD

The special education placement of children, as a result of federal and state legislation, has consumed increasing amounts of time and energy for regular and special educators. In this case, state law requires that each identified handicapped child, ages three to twenty-one, be provided with a free and appropriate educational program in accordance with the child's individualized education program (IEP). The state statute is patterned after comparable federal legislation. As you consider your responses to the placement problem revealed in the documents that follow, please view the entire matter from the perspective of each of the following positions:

> principal of Maize Village School
> director of special education
> superintendent of schools
> executive director of M.E.E.D.
> superintendent of the Martin Zone Center

In light of the law, can insufficient space or funds be a legitimate reason to exclude an otherwise eligible child for special education services? Why or why not? How could each position better contribute to a satisfactory solution to the problem than what the letters/memoranda indicate? Should the parents have started with the public schools instead of private agencies to obtain an appropriate placement for their son? Why or why not? Who should they have contacted first? In the end, which of the positions must be responsible for the child's placement? Where will the buck stop?

MEMORANDUM

To: M. J. Johnson, Superintendent

From: P. F. Loock, Director of Special Education

Subject: File re: Jones, John Wm.

Enclosed is a file of materials I've gathered after receiving the letter and enclosures from Ira Best, Principal of the Maize Village Elementary School. I thought that I'd better send it up to you since Ira indicates that the parents may want to appeal this decision not to admit their son to our pilot class at his school. We don't know yet if they will request a formal case study and then a complete IEP.

This is not the first case we've had this year of requests for admission after we'd fill the class. I think the Jones' case is fairly typical of parents who do not accept institutionalization of their child and seek various sorts of community assistance.

How should we handle the Joneses? Should we do a case study on our own initiative?

enc.

MEMORANDUM

To: P. F. Loock, Director of Special Education

From: I. M. Best, Principal

Subject: John Williams JONES, III (CA 4–2)

Mrs. Mary Jones of 1234 Apple Way came into my office yesterday (Monday, the third) to enroll her son, John, in our pilot class for the preschool handicapped. It seems that Miss Sneed of the M.E.E.D. school recommended that she seek to have her son placed here (see photocopy of letter from her—attached).

I tried hard to assure Mrs. Jones of our concern for her son's proper development, but the pilot class was full and we did not anticipate that additional classes would be available until the next school year. In addition, from what I could see of her son's behavior, we could probably not take him anyway in that his hyperactivity would require more attention than would be possible, given the present enrollment and just one teacher and aide. Mrs. Jones said she did not have an IEP for John. She had not heard of an IEP before.

When I suggested that Mrs. Jones investigate the Martin Zone Center as an alternative placement, she became rather agitated and incoherent—finally producing the letter I have photocopied and attached hereto. It seems that the Joneses have spent considerable time in phoning, visiting, writing to public and private agencies who refer them to someone else.

Frankly, I think the Joneses have had it! They are ready to do something drastic, and I think they know enough about the law to insist that their son is eligible for special educational services. I suspect that you will be their next "target" as Mrs. Jones obtained your name and Dr. Johnson's.

The Jones boy is another example of our need for more classes of this type and for a better teacher/pupil ratio.

enc. (2)

Martin City Education for the Emotionally Disturbed

A United Fund Agency

Mr. and Mrs. James Jones
1234 Apple Way
Martin City, N.C. 69999

Dear Mr. and Mrs. Jones:

This is to confirm our recent telephone conversation concerning your son, John. I wish it were possible for me to give you good news, but the facts remain: we have funds for just fifteen children, and John is third on the waiting list. As I indicated, some parents have had to wait for as long as two and one-half years before space became available.

I just checked with United Fund headquarters and learned that they were not hopeful regarding our request for additional funds as contributions in the last drive were less than anticipated. Thus we are unable to estimate when a vacancy will occur to provide for John's admission to our program.

Have you checked with the Martin City Schools? I understand that they have recently initiated a pilot class for handicapped preschool children, for which John might be eligible. The class is located in the nearby Maize Village Elementary School.

Very truly yours,

B. A. Sneed
Executive Director
M.E.E.D.

cc: Principal, Maize Village School

MARTIN ZONE CENTER

N.C. State Department of Mental Health
P. O. Box 007
Martin City, N.C.

In answering refer to: MZC/DMH: AJ/abc

Dear Mr. and Mrs. Jones:

This is to acknowledge your inquiry regarding services available at the Center for your son, John Williams Jones, III (CA 4).

We have examined the materials you sent us and regret to inform you that your son is not eligible for services at this time. Due to lack of sufficient space and staff, we have been forced to limit admissions to children aged five or older.

Providing that our budget request (currently being considered for the next fiscal year) is acted upon favorably, it may be possible to provide limited (maximum two weeks) respite care for John, starting in September. For further information regarding this program, please contact us sometime during this coming summer.

Another possible community resource for John might be the M.E.E.D. School. While designed primarily for emotionally disturbed children, your son's lack of speech and the equivocal nature of the diagnosis at this time should insure eligibility for enrollment. Ms. B. A. Sneed is the Director of the M.E.E.D. School which is located at 9999 Middle Road (Phone: 555–6553).

We hope that this will be helpful to you in finding the needed services for your son.

Sincerely yours,

A. Friend, M.D.
Superintendent

by: A. J. Pung, Ph.D.
Staff Psychologist II

Mr. and Mrs. James Jones
1234 Apple Way
Martin City, N.C. 69999

QUESTIONS FOR DISCUSSION

1. As the principal in this case, would you recommend the school district take the initiative or wait to see what the parents do next? Why?
2. What would district policy most likely be in a case like this?
3. How would a human resources perspective differ from a strict adherence to the "letter of the law" in special education?

CASE STUDY NUMBER 4

A FEMALE PRINCIPAL TRIES FOR A PROMOTION

Scottstown Elementary School District, which is experiencing growth, has 2950 students in five buildings.

School	Enrollment	Principal	Years as Principal
McBride	900	Mrs. Jay	18, retiring
Macauley	600	Mr. Queue	9
McPherson	550	Ms. Arrh	9
MacDonald	450	Mr. Ess	6
McDougall	450	Ms. Teah	4

The vacancy at McBride Elementary School was advertised on March 15 in the local newspaper, appropriate college placement services, and the state administrators' bulletin. As usual, the equal opportunity and affirmative action employer statement was included. Seventy-five people applied for the position, including three district principals, Ms. Arrh, Mr. Ess, and Ms. Teah. Since McBride Elementary School was the newest and largest school in the district with a higher salary going to its principal, the district's principals viewed the position as a promotion.

The school board had a farewell cocktail party for Mrs. Jay on April 5. This party was attended by all board members, the principals and central office staff. During the party, Mr. Queue, a close friend of Ms. Arrh, overheard the chairman of the board tell another board member, "As far as I'm concerned, the vacant position will be offered to a man. We have enough women principals, we don't need another pushy female in our biggest elementary school."

During the week of April 28, the three top candidates for the principalship were announced, and interviews were held. The candidates were the following:

1) Mr. Yu, of Japanese descent, has been an assistant principal in a neighboring district for five years. While he has been successful, it is known that some parents feel highly dissatisfied with his work.

2) Mr. Veih is principal of a rural school downstate that is closing. He has served there well for three years under trying circumstances. He has an excellent recommendation from his superintendent.

3) Ms. Arrh is principal of McPherson School. She has always had excellent evaluations by her staff and by the superintendent. She operates democratically with the faculty in decision making. She is well liked by the children and by the parents. During her nine years at McPherson, teacher turnover has been minimal, with three consecutive years of no staff changes during that time. She has worked closely with faculty and parents to improve the reading and mathematics programs. During the past five years, the average achievement scores in these two areas have risen significantly.

At the end of the three days of interviewing, the faculty and the parent leaders of McBride School voted almost unanimously to recommend hiring Ms. Arrh. At the school board meeting on May 8 and after an initial discussion about the candidates among the board members, the board members decided that a straw vote should be taken to see if they could get a unanimous vote in the open meeting later. The board chairman insisted on this method because he believed that if the board did not choose Ms. Arrh, the vote should be unanimous. The board went into a closed executive session with the superintendent. The straw vote showed that there was unanimity on offering the position to Mr. Yu.

The school board consisted of one woman and four men. All of the board members were known to be outspoken opponents of the ERA movement. The sexist remark of the board chairman at the cocktail party was common knowledge. The district has no racial or ethnic minorities persons in any central office position or building administration position.

QUESTIONS FOR DISCUSSION

1. Should Ms. Arrh have taken any action prior to the straw vote in executive session? Should the elementary principals as a group have taken any action?
2. If you were Ms. Arrh, what, if anything, could you have done before the formal vote of the board was taken in the open meeting? Could the elementary principals as a group have done anything?
3. What are the implications of any decision made by the school board in this case?
4. What would you assume about the superintendent's role in all of this? Why?
5. Does the input from a selection committee deserve serious consideration? Is it binding? What are the morale implications of rejecting it?
6. Would a human resources approach always preclude bringing in outside people for promotions? Why or why not?

CASE STUDY NUMBER 5

MASTER AGREEMENT WOES

The principals of the West Bend Elementary School District were at their weekly get-together. Rather than discuss local administrative practices and review a recent periodical article on either administration or supervision, the pre-determined topic was the recently negotiated collective bargaining agreement between the school board and the local teachers' association.

John Thomas was disgusted, "I can't believe that the school board realized the effect the new contract will have on the administration of the schools in this district."

"You're right. That contract ties our hands in a number of ways." Ed Wright was glum.

John lamented, "What really ticks me off is that the teachers have obtained the right to determine by majority vote whether the kids get to go outside for recess in inclement weather. They apparently get to vote in the morning before school starts and give their decision to the principal through their association building representative. And what about the provision that allows teachers to go home five minutes after the kids leave in the afternoon unless there is a faculty meeting which the contract says we can call only once a month unless the teachers agree to have more than one meeting."

John caught his breath and continued, "These contract provisions will do nothing but strain our working relationships with the faculties in our schools!"

Ed chimed in, "Just yesterday, Ginny Wunderlich asked for permission to leave fifteen minutes early so that she could have her hair done before an early dinner-date. I covered her class beginning at 3 o'clock, and she left. Can you imagine that happening under this new master contract? I'm sure that Ginny and the other teachers at my school don't know that I won't be able to continue such practices. We'll have to stick to the letter of the master agreement." With his voice nearly breaking, Ed concluded, "Before this agreement, teachers were supposed to stay in the building until 4 P.M. Now they can leave at 3:20. We won't have any flexibility to stretch policies to help someone out as we did in the past."

Ernie Franks took a deep breath, "I just can't imagine that the school board really wants this. I think the board was really pressured by the local union leaders, not the rank and file of the teachers. Why, only one third of the teachers in my building belong to the teachers' association. Most of the others don't even realize that they will now have to pay dues to the association whether they are members or not. That's the so-called new 'fair share' provision!"

Lisa Clayton said, "I'm worried about the strict labor-management position that we will be in with this new agreement. Here we are, elementary principals with no voice in the negotiations process. The school board did not solicit input from us on association demands and the board's counterproposals. But guess who will have to administer the master agreement at the building level?"

Ed intoned, "That means, of course, we principals become the fall guys, the ones who will get slapped with grievances and building representative lectures on 'proper' interpretation of the agreement."

"See what I mean," Lisa shouted. "No matter what, we are in the middle of the mess! Don't forget, Ed, the superintendent or the school board won't get the grievances for supposedly violating contract provisions. The least the board can do is brief us on how to interpret some of the language in this new agreement."

Ernie cried, "I can't believe this has happened to us! What can we do?"

QUESTIONS FOR DISCUSSION

1. What are the principals' options in this situation?
2. How can the principals work with the master agreement and still keep good professional relationships with the faculty?
3. Have these principals based their concerns on facts or fears?

4. Should the elementary principals become members of the board's negotiating team and confront teacher association representatives at the negotiating table? If not, how can they gain some role in the negotiations process?

5. What attributes of "excellence" from Peters and Waterman's conclusions about highly successful organizations were in jeopardy here?

6. Some say that unions are incompatible with educational purposes? What do you think? What lessons can schools learn from business in this regard?

7. How could these principals turn an apparent win/lose situation into a win/win situation for all concerned parties?

CASE STUDY NUMBER 6	DECISION TIME ON SCHOOL USE BY OUTSIDE GROUPS

The Nodaway Unified School District has 15,000 students in most of Eleazer County. There are three elementary schools and one high school located within the city limits of Nodaway. The other schools are located in various parts of the quite heavily populated county.

The Flanders Elementary School has rarely had requests for use of the school building by groups not associated with the public school system. The principal of Flanders suddenly received five requests to use building facilities. The requests had come from the local boy scout troop, the First United Church, Older Citizens United for Rights, a Flanders teacher, and a sex therapy group.

After reading the letters of request, the principal checked the school board's policy handbook to find the policy on the use of the district's school buildings by outside groups. To the principal's amazement, the policy simply stated that the principal of each building shall use his or her good judgment in allowing outside groups to use building facilities so long as the school's regular educational program is not interrupted. The principal, P. J. Buckmaster, immediately contacted the other two city Nodaway elementary school principals for advice only to learn that they, too, were receiving requests for building use by the elderly, religious groups, and profit-making organizations.

In view of the broad policy on building use and the potential for abuse inherent in some requests, Principal Buckmaster and colleagues have become quite concerned and uneasy about approving any of the requests. In the meantime, P. J. Buckmaster will be expected to respond to each of the five requests on the principal's desk.

The Boy Scouts of America
Troop 115
Nodaway, N.C.

P. J. Buckmaster, Principal
Flanders Elementary School
Nodaway Unified School District
914 West Tara
Nodaway, N.C.

Dear P. J.:

This is a request for permission to use the cafeteria in Flanders School for our weekly troop meeting every Wednesday night from 7 to 9 P.M.

As you know, we have met ever since our founding in the recreation room of the First United Church. Since they are demolishing the building in order to rebuild on the same site, we must locate in other quarters. We have searched the city and have been unable to find an available suitable facility except for the elementary building.

We will need to begin using the cafeteria on June 1. I imagine that we will meet there for approximately a year and a half before moving back to the new church building.

Sincerely yours,

Scott Johnson, Scoutmaster

SJ:der

First United Church
Nodaway, N.C.

P. J. Buckmaster, Principal
Flanders Elementary School
914 West Tara
Nodaway, N.C.

Dear Principal Buckmaster:

Our congregation has decided to build a new sanctuary and
hopes to have it completed within a year. Since we must raze our
present edifice, it will be necessary for our flock to worship elsewhere until the new building has been completed and dedicated.

This is a request for permission to use the Flanders elementary
school gymnasium for worship services beginning on June 5. We
would like to rent it on Sunday mornings from 8 until noon and also
on Wednesday evenings from 8 until 9:30 P.M.

Since we have a rather large Sunday School, we would also like
to rent ten classrooms on Sunday mornings from 9 to 10 A.M.

May we hear from you soon?

Sincerely,

Rev. Jess Todd
Senior Pastor

JT:am

OLDER CITIZENS UNITED FOR RIGHTS
214 East North Street
Nodaway, N.C.

Principal Buckmaster:

At the last meeting of O.C.U.R., we were delighted to read the superintendent's letter saying that you have agreed to let us meet in the cafeteria of Flanders School on Monday nights.

We were less elated, however, about the rumored refusal to let us use a classroom to meet every day beginning at 10:00 A.M. We know there are three vacant classrooms at Flanders. Don't you realize we are all retired and need a place to call our own during the day? There is simply no other convenient place we can meet in this city.

We want you and the school board to consider this request again. We want all board members to remember that we have known them for years and that this apparent refusal is no way for them to turn against us older folks.

Bertha Jasins, President

BJ:er

Jean Arthur Cummings
1214 South Parkway
Nodaway, N.C.

P. J. Buckmaster, Principal
Flanders Elementary School
914 West Tara Place
Nodaway, N.C.

Dear P. J.:

Before coming to the Nodaway District as a teacher two years ago, I was an instructor in aerobic dancing for the continuing education program of the district in which I taught.

Many of the people in Nodaway have asked me to start an aerobic dancing class here. I am willing to do this, but since we do not have a continuing education program to sponsor such a class, I will have to charge a fee to the participants.

I would like to hold classes from 7:00 to 9:00 P.M. every Wednesday next fall, from September 1 through December 15.

P. J., I hope that you will grant this request.

Sincerely,

Jean Arthur Cummings
Teacher, Grade 5
Flanders School

JAC:rd

SELF REALIZATION THROUGH SEX THERAPY
A Nonprofit Organization
Federally Funded
State University of N.C.

P. J. Buckmaster, Principal
Flanders Elementary School
914 West Tara Place
Nodaway, N.C.

Dear Principal Buckmaster:

Self Realization Through Sex Therapy is coming to Nodaway! More than 1,000 people have taken our course in six cities of our state alone! Our methods are known to produce happier people and happier marriages. Now this can happen, too, to the citizens of Nodaway.

We plan to conduct four twelve week sessions during the next year, from September 1 through August 30. In order to do this, we would like to rent the Flanders Elementary School gymnasium or lunchroom every Wednesday evening from 6:00 to 10:00 P.M.

I know that our program has caused quite a stir in the state. Let me assure you, however, that our methods of instruction are basically lecture and audio-visual. We will need the use of gym mats for relaxation exercises.

Our charge to participants is $100 per single or $150 per couple. We limit enrollment to twenty people per twelve week session.

I hope you and your wife will participate in our sessions. We will be happy to have you attend as our guests.

Thank you,

John and Mary Jordon
Sex Therapy Unit
State University of N.C.

J&MJ:rde

QUESTIONS FOR DISCUSSION

1. What should Principal Buckmaster and the other principals do next?
2. Should unilateral action be taken or withheld until the principals can meet together to develop a unified approach?
3. How would the superintendent view Principal Buckmaster's reluctance to make decisions on these requests?
4. Should the school board be informed?
5. If you were asked by the superintendent to submit a list of items to be considered for the development of a written policy for the district, what would be on your list?
6. What community trend might these requests indicate? How can the school system respond without simply reacting?

CASE STUDY NUMBER 7

TOO MANY FORCES!

The Urban Town School Board recently and unanimously decided to change its organizational structure to a highly decentralized system. The board set up site-based management in all of the schools after a year of transition and training of administrators and teachers. The Board decided to give the local school councils great powers over the governance of local schools. Among these powers was the hiring and firing of principals, introducing curriculum opportunities and the use of Chapter I money. The local elementary school councils each had six parents, two community members, two teachers representatives, and the principal. All council members were elected by their constituencies except the school principal. The overall purpose of the local school council was to improve the quality of education.

Jack Shepp, a nonminority principal, had been administering the grades five through eight Leslie Middle School for thirteen years. The ethnic breakdown of the large school was 6 percent white, 15 percent black and 78 percent Hispanic. The majority of the students were overage and scored below national norms in reading and math. The student mobility rate for the school was 42 percent. The graduation rate for eighth graders last year was 60 percent.

Most of the parents, community organizations, students, and staff supported the principal. A majority in the local school council (6–4) voted to issue a contract to Mr. Shepp for four years. This vote has been in litigation because the four dissenting members believed certain required procedures were not followed. These same four members, three parents and a community representative, viciously campaigned against the school principal and his ideas to improve the school. This group had become highly visible in the community and the local media. They said the students were not achieving at national norms. Mr. Shepp had not done anything to improve the educational quality at the school in his thirteen years there. The principal offered statistics that showed the school was equivalent in academic standings to similar schools in inner city areas.

Some teachers and parents believed that underlying the parents protests, including a hunger strike to get the principal removed, was their desire to get a Hispanic principal. Recently the school's Hispanic teachers and an assistant principal had joined the four dissenting local school council members.

At the school many faculty members had become aware of some problems that existed among the bilingual education teachers. There were eight teachers representing several academic areas. There was a lead teacher and a bilingual coordinator, assigned by the central office, who supervised these teachers.

This supervisory arrangement had caused excessive conflict and tension. The bilingual coordinator was responsible for such duties as insuring that the program was fulfilling the state requirements, verifying that necessary forms were completed and accurate, supplying materials and ordering equipment and providing instructional leadership. The coordinator was excellent in handling the paper requirements of the job. She was not supportive of the principal and felt that the school should have a principal who speaks Spanish. She had become vindictive to other bilingual teachers who did not support her view. She had denied them access to materials, to the more desirable rooms, threatened the loss of a job to untenured personnel, disregarded faculty recommendations, failed to provide aid and leadership to new faculty, and became inaccessible to the teachers who supported the principal. Furthermore, there had been a large number of transfer requests by the bilingual teachers.

Another area of the school was also facing some difficulties that may have had political ramifications for the principal. Three computer science teachers shared the computer laboratory. The Hispanic teacher was always complaining that when he came into the room the computers were not working, the chalkboard was full of graffiti, and there was vandalism done to the printers. The other two non-Hispanic teachers had complained to the principal about the Hispanic teacher. They said he was the cause of the broken and vandalized computer equipment because he did not supervise the students.

Jack Shepp's school was the only one in the school district embroiled in so much site-based management controversy. Indeed, the School Board continually heard complaints from other district schools that the problems at Leslie Middle School could jeopardize the entire policy of site-based management in the school district. One board member was now against the continuation of site-based management in the school district.

QUESTIONS FOR DISCUSSION

1. How important is ethnicity or gender in selecting a principal? Does your answer hold up for all groups and locations in the United States?
2. Should the principal use a human relations or a human resources approach with the local school council? Explain your choice. Should he try a win/win or a win/lose negotiations strategy? Explain your answer.
3. Should the principal do anything about the assistant principal who is supportive of the four dissenting local school council members? The nonsupportive bilingual coordinator? Should he find a "linking pin" on the staff to help him deal with the assistant principal and Hispanic teachers? Why or why not?
4. How would you manage the problems among the bilingual and computer science teachers? What contingency leadership model or factors would you consider here? Would ethnicity be one of the factors? Why or why not?
5. Could knowledge of the decision rules be helpful to the principal here? Why or why not?
6. In this case, can the conflicts at Leslie Middle School be managed in isolation from the rest of the school district? Why or why not? How could the principal turn the complaints from other district schools to his advantage in managing the conflicts at his school?

Simulation exercise: Members of the class may each be assigned a role (local council member, principal, bilingual coordinator, computer science teacher, assistant principal, school board member, concerned administrator from another school, etc.). The goal would be to minimize the problems existing at the middle school so that the site-based management experiment could continue in all schools.

REFERENCES

Carl Ashbaugh and Katherine Kasten, **Educational Leadership: Case Studies for Reflective Practice** (White Plains, NY: Longman Publishing, 1991).

Warren Bennis, **Why Leaders Can't Lead: The Unconscious Conspiracy Continues** (San Francisco: Jossey-Bass, 1989).

Arthur Blumberg, **School Administration as Craft: Foundations of Practice** (Boston: Allyn & Bacon, Inc., 1988).

Daniel J. Brown, **Decentralization: The Administrator's Guidebook to School District Change** (Newbury Park, CA: Corwin Press, Inc., 1991).

Carl D. Glickman, "Pushing School Reform to a New Edge: The Seven Ironies of School Empowerment," **Phi Delta Kappan** 72, No. 1 (September, 1990): 68–75.

Laurence Iannaccone and Frank W. Lutz, **Politics, Power and Policy: The Governing of Local School Districts** (Columbus, Ohio: Charles E. Merrill, 1970).

Anne Lewis, **Restructuring America's Schools** (Arlington, VA: American Association of School Administrators, 1989).

James M. Lipham, Robb E. Rankin, and James A. Hoeh, Jr., **The Principalship: Concepts, Competencies, and Cases** (New York: Longman, Inc., 1985).

Paul E. Peterson, **School Politics Chicago Style** (Chicago: The University of Chicago Press, 1976).

Ronald W. Rebore, **Educational Administration: A Management Approach** (Englewood Cliffs, N.J.: Prentice-Hall, Inc., 1985).

Thomas J. Sergiovanni, Martin Burlingame, Fred S. Coombs and Paul W. Thurston, **Educational Governance and Administration** (Englewood Cliffs, N.J.: Prentice-Hall, 1980). See especially Chapter 5, "Policy-Making In The Local School District," pp. 127–151.

H. Rutherford Turnbull and Ann Turnbull, **Free Appropriate Public Education: Law and Implementation** (Denver: Love Publishing Co., 1978).

Gregory R. Weisenstein and Ruth Pelz, **Administrator's Desk Reference on Special Education** (Rockville, MD: Aspen Publishers, Inc., 1986).

Frederick M. Wirt and Michael W. Kirst, **Schools in Conflict,** 2nd ed. (Berkeley: McCutchan Publishing Corp., 1989).

Harmon L. Ziegler and M. Kent Jennings with G. Wayne Peak, **Governing American Public Schools: Political Interaction in Local School Districts** (North Scituate, Massachusetts: Duxbury Press, 1974).

INDEX